American Social Thought

OTHER BOOKS BY RAY GINGER

The Bending Cross: A Biography of Eugene Victor Debs
Six Days or Forever?: Tennessee versus John Thomas Scopes
Altgeld's America: The Lincoln Ideal versus Changing Realities

American Social Thought

Edited by RAY GINGER

Brandeis University

American Century Series

 HILL AND WANG – NEW YORK

Preface

IN HIS famous essay "Genius, Fame, and the Comparison of Races," Charles Horton Cooley argued that the general spirit prevailing at a given time and place tends to direct the energies of the most able men into a few definite channels. He pointed to the fantastic output of great painting and sculpture in Italy around 1500; of great dramatic writing in Elizabethan England. This volume can serve as another demonstration of Cooley's argument, for in the years around 1900 a large proportion of the Americans of incisive consciousness took up the task of revamping social theory.

The twelve persons whose work is sampled here can justly be regarded as members of a single generation. The oldest was Peirce, born in 1839; the youngest, Cooley and Ross, were both born the year after Appomattox. Even this assertion understates the degree of concentration. Peirce, Holmes, and James were all born between 1839 and 1842, moved in the same social circles in Boston, and belonged for some years to the same discussion group. The other nine were born in a span of seventeen years, beginning with Gompers in 1850. Dewey grew up on a Vermont farm, Gompers in London and New York, but the others all came from farms or towns around the Great Lakes. During the period that concerns us six of these men served on the faculty of a large midwestern university: Dewey and Veblen at Chicago; Cooley at Michigan; Commons, Turner, and Ross at Wisconsin.

Similarly, the selections given were published in quite rapid sequence, from Turner's "The Significance of the Frontier" in 1893 to Veblen's "Intellectual Pre-eminence of Jews" in 1919. Omitting the last from consideration, each of the others appeared between 1893 and 1908.

So one criterion in selecting an essay for this book was that it seemed a representative work by a member of a certain generation, published during the years around 1900. When I say representative, of course I do not mean most representative. Many of Veblen's main ideas do not figure explicitly in the essay reprinted here. Peirce's sustained effort to work out the techniques of logic that would "make our ideas clear" does not appear in his discourse on "The Century's Great Men of Science." Dewey is more honored now as a philosopher than as a pedagogue. Nonetheless each selection here can be taken as fairly typical of its author's work in that it deals with a type of problem that interested him and also shows the mental stance from which he sliced into problems. Veblen is sly and ironic. The three Bostonians are witty and eloquent. Dewey is earnest. Cooley can seem almost platitudinous until he suddenly makes you aware that the implications of his offhand remarks are contrary to beliefs you hold and have never bothered to question. Save for the labor leaders Debs and Gompers and the social worker Jane Addams, these authors were all academics. Peirce is another apparent exception, since he served on a university faculty only briefly and at low rank. But he was a trained scientist, competent in physics as well as philosophy, and his chief occupation of writing for encyclopedias can justly be regarded as intellectual work. At least, the way Peirce did it it can.

So much for what we might call the technical grounds of selection. Now for the more substantive ones. First, significance. Every selection seems to me to raise issues of the first importance to understanding of human nature and its relations to the social order. In our own day we have become accustomed to articles, often based on laborious research, that raise questions so trivial that the article cannot possibly mean very much to readers and perhaps did not mean very much to its author. In contrast, the essays here cope with theoretical problems of wide import and each of them—for all the pithy examples they contain—operates on a pretty high level of abstraction.

I have also been guided by a desire to give the book a measure of unity. Therefore I have so chosen the essays, and so arranged them in sequence, that questions raised in one selection are viewed from a different perspective or probed into more deeply in later selections. James' essay, for example, suggests itself as a highly usable basis for a system of ethics. But James himself chose to set it in another context, saying: "The two questions, first, that of the possible extent of our powers; and, second, that of the various avenues of approach to them, the various keys for unlocking them in diverse individuals, dominate the whole problem of individual and national education." So I have placed Dewey's contribution next, for he uses a similar point of view to criticize the schools that existed and to suggest improvements. Next, Veblen holds that the chief characteristic of a scientist is his skepticism, and then Peirce singles out idle curiosity as the quality distinguishing great nineteenth-century scientists from their predecessors. Turner argues that the succession of American frontiers propagated democracy, while Cooley mentions that they have intensified competition. How far, as who would ask, can these last two propositions be reduced to a single thesis? And so on. You will find many other places where one of these essays plays off in an illuminating way upon another.

As these examples show, the essays resemble each other in trying to elucidate what Veblen called "the massive forces working obscurely in the background." But they are not for that reason themselves obscure or ponderous. Far from it. Each paper is a self-contained argument, and each can be read by anybody who cares to explore its subject. No specialized background or vocabulary is needed. In those more profound and less pretentious times, the best scholars aimed at making their meaning accessible to all who could read the vocabulary and the types of discourse which any educated person of the time could read. William James did not write in a jargon known only to psychologists, nor did Holmes bother much with those legal phrases that are insubstantial as cotton candy, nor does Cooley appear before us in the impersonal robes of sociology and speak a tongue available only to a few other members of his mystical guild. Veblen may seem an exception, but he never used a language peculiar to social anthropology —he wrote in a language peculiar to himself. It was often convoluted, but it was good prose by the highest test of all: It was effective as a means of communicating *his* meaning.

The thought applies to all the authors represented in this book.

If these men were great as expounders of American social thought, a good part of the reason is that each of them dared to be himself. Far from equating objectivity with impersonality, each of them parades his own ideas and tries to convince us of his own conclusions. As a result these essays carry a zest and passion seldom met with in scholarly writing. And a humor: readers who are consumed always by serious-mindedness will miss much here that has delighted others. But all readers of these essays might properly say of every one: "Who touches this work touches a man." These days, that is a good deal to say.

Because I meant the body of this book to contain only good writing, I wanted to use everything in the exact form in which the author wrote it. I have not succeeded even in a majority of instances, but my deletions with a blue pencil have been minor and do not, I trust, work violence on the ideas of any of the authors.

The pages that follow contain much enlightenment and stimulation; I think that readers, for that reason and for the frequent charm of statement, will have fun reading them.

RAY GINGER

Brandeis University
March 1961

Contents

ix

CONTENTS

American Social Thought

The Energies of Men

WILLIAM JAMES

William James (1842–1910) was born in New York City but received much of his early schooling in Europe. He considered becoming a painter, but his philosopher father urged upon him a "less narrowing" career in science. James was granted his medical degree by Harvard and became an instructor in physiology there. When he instituted the first course in this country in the exciting new field of physiological psychology, publisher Henry Holt asked him to write a textbook on the subject. James' *Principles of Psychology* was published in two volumes in 1890 and is still highly regarded more than seventy years later; a recent poll of psychologists in the United States singled out James as the most important American in the history of the discipline. But his own interests drifted increasingly to philosophy, and in 1897 his title at Harvard was changed to Professor of Philosophy. This essay was his presidential address to the American Philosophical Association in 1906, as revised and published in his *Essays on Faith and Morals* (New York: Longmans, Green, 1949), printed here by permission of Paul R. Reynolds & Son and John Farquharson, Ltd.

EVERYONE KNOWS what it is to start a piece of work, either intellectual or muscular, feeling stale—or *oold*, as an Adirondack guide once put it to me. And everybody knows what it is to "warm up" to his job. The process of warming up gets particularly striking in the phenomenon known as "second wind." On usual occasions we make a practice of stopping an occupation as soon as we meet the first effective layer (so to call it) of fatigue. We have then

1

walked, played, or worked "enough," so we desist. That amount of
fatigue is an efficacious obstruction on this side of which our usual
life is cast. But if an unusual necessity forces us to press onward,
a surprising thing occurs. The fatigue gets worse up to a certain
critical point, when gradually or suddenly it passes away, and we
are fresher than before. We have evidently tapped a level of new
energy, masked until then by the fatigue-obstacle usually obeyed.
There may be layer after layer of this experience. A third and a
fourth "wind" may supervene. Mental activity shows the phenomenon as well as physical, and in exceptional cases we may find,
beyond the very extremity of fatigue-distress, amounts of ease and
power that we never dreamed ourselves to own,—sources of
strength habitually not taxed at all, because habitually we never
push through the obstruction, never pass those early critical points.

For many years I have mused on the phenomenon of second
wind, trying to find a physiological theory. It is evident that our
organism has stored-up reserves of energy that are ordinarily not
called upon, but that may be called upon: deeper and deeper
strata of combustible or explosible material, discontinuously arranged, but ready for use by anyone who probes so deep, and
repairing themselves by rest as well as do the superficial strata.
Most of us continue living unnecessarily near our surface. Our
energy-budget is like our nutritive budget. Physiologists say that
a man is in "nutritive equilibrium" when day after day he neither
gains nor loses weight. But the odd thing is that this condition may
obtain on astonishingly different amounts of food. Take a man in
nutritive equilibrium, and systematically increase or lessen his
rations. In the first case he will begin to gain weight, in the second
case to lose it. The change will be the greatest on the first day,
less on the second, less still on the third; and so on, till he has
gained all that he will gain, or lost all that he will lose, on that
altered diet. He is now in nutritive equilibrium again, but with a
new weight; and this neither lessens nor increases because his
various combustion processes have adjusted themselves to the
changed dietary. He gets rid, in one way or another, of just as
much N,C,H, etc., as he takes in *per diem*.

Just so one can be in what I might call "efficiency-equilibrium"
(neither gaining nor losing power when once the equilibrium is

reached) on astonishingly different quantities of work, no matter in what direction the work may be measured. It may be physical work, intellectual work, moral work, or spiritual work.

Of course there are limits: the trees don't grow into the sky. But the plain fact remains that men the world over possess amounts of resource which only very exceptional individuals push to their extremes of use. But the very same individual, pushing his energies to their extreme, may in a vast number of cases keep the pace up day after day, and find no "reaction" of a bad sort, so long as decent hygienic conditions are preserved. His more active rate of energizing does not wreck him; for the organism adapts itself, and as the rate of waste augments, augments correspondingly the rate of repair.

I say the *rate* and not the *time* of repair. The busiest man needs no more hours of rest than the idler. Some years ago Professor Patrick, of the Iowa State University, kept three young men awake for four days and nights. When his observations on them were finished, the subjects were permitted to sleep themselves out. All awoke from this sleep completely refreshed, but the one who took the longest to restore himself from his long vigil only slept one-third more time than was regular with him.

If my reader will put together these two conceptions, first, that few men live at their maximum of energy, and second, that anyone may be in vital equilibrium at very different rates of energizing, he will find, I think, that a very pretty practical problem of national economy, as well as of individual ethics, opens upon his view. In rough terms, we may say that a man who energizes below his normal maximum fails by just so much to profit by his chance at life; and that a nation filled with such men is inferior to a nation run at higher pressure. The problem is, then, how can men be trained up to their most useful pitch of energy? And how can nations make such training most accessible to all their sons and daughters? This, after all, is only the general problem of education, formulated in slightly different terms.

"Rough" terms, I said just now, because the words "energy" and "maximum" may easily suggest only *quantity* to the reader's mind, whereas in measuring the human energies of which I speak, qualities as well as quantities have to be taken into account. Everyone feels that his total *power* rises when he passes to a higher qualitative level of life.

Writing is higher than walking, thinking is higher than writing, deciding higher than thinking, deciding "no" higher than deciding "yes"—at least the man who passes from one of these activities to another will usually say that each later one involves a greater element of *inner work* than the earlier ones, even though the total heat given out or the foot-pounds expended by the organism may be less. Just how to conceive this inner work physiologically is as yet impossible, but psychologically we all know what the word means. We need a particular spur or effort to start us upon inner work; it tires us to sustain it; and when long sustained, we know how easily we lapse. When I speak of "energizing," and its rates and levels and sources, I mean therefore our inner as well as our outer work.

Let no one think, then, that our problem of individual and national economy is solely that of the maximum of pounds raisable against gravity, the maximum of locomotion, or of agitation of any sort that human beings can accomplish. That might signify little more than hurrying and jumping about in uncoordinated ways; whereas inner work, though it so often reinforces outer work, quite as often means its arrest. To relax, to say to ourselves (with the "new thoughters") "Peace! be still!" is sometimes a great achievement of inner work. When I speak of human energizing in general, the reader must therefore understand that sum-total of activities, some outer and some inner, some muscular, some emotional, some moral, some spiritual, of whose waxing and waning in himself he is at all times so well aware. How to keep it at an appreciable maximum? How not to let the level lapse? That is the great problem. But the work of men and women is of innumerable kinds, each kind being, as we say, carried on by a particular faculty; so the great problem splits into two sub-problems thus:

1. What are the limits of human faculty in various directions?

2. By what diversity of means, in the differing types of human beings, may the faculties be stimulated to their best results?

Read in one way, these two questions sound both trivial and familiar: there is a sense in which we have all asked them ever since we were born. Yet *as a methodical program of scientific inquiry,* I doubt whether they have ever been seriously taken up. If answered fully, almost the whole of mental science and of the science of conduct would find a place under them. I propose, in what follows, to press them on the reader's attention in an informal way.

The first point to agree upon in this enterprise is that *as a rule men habitually use only a small part of the powers which they actually possess and which they might use under appropriate conditions.*

Everyone is familiar with the phenomenon of feeling more or less alive on different days. Everyone knows on any given day that there are energies slumbering in him which the incitements of that day do not call forth, but which he might display if these were greater. Most of us feel as if a sort of cloud weighed upon us, keeping us below our highest notch of clearness in discernment, sureness in reasoning, or firmness in deciding. Compared with what we ought to be, we are only half awake. Our fires are damped, our drafts are checked. We are making use of only a small part of our possible mental and physical resources. In some persons this sense of being cut off from their rightful resources is extreme, and we then get the formidable neurasthenic and psychasthenic conditions, with life grown into one tissue of impossibilities, that so many medical books describe.

Stating the thing broadly, the human individual thus lives usually far within his limits; he possesses powers of various sorts which he habitually fails to use. He energizes below his *maximum,* and he behaves below his *optimum.* In elementary faculty, in coordination, in power of *inhibition* and control, in every conceivable way, his life is contracted like the field of vision of a hysteric subject— but with less excuse, for the poor hysteric is diseased, while in the rest of us it is only an inveterate *habit*—the habit of inferiority to our full self—that is bad.

Admit so much, then, and admit also that the charge of being inferior to their full self is far truer of some men than of others; then the practical question ensues: *to what do the better men owe their escape? and, in the fluctuations which all men feel in their own degree of energizing, to what are the improvements due, when they occur?*

In general terms the answer is plain:

Either some unusual stimulus fills them with emotional excitement, or some unusual idea of necessity induces them to make an extra effort of will. *Excitements, ideas, and efforts,* in a word, are what carry us over the dam.

In those "hyperesthetic" conditions which chronic invalidism so often brings in its train, the dam has changed its normal place. The slightest functional exercise gives a distress which the patient yields to and stops. In such cases of "habit-neurosis" a new range of power often comes in consequence of the "bullying-treatment," of efforts which the doctor obliges the patient, much against his will, to make. First comes the very extremity of distress, then follows unexpected relief. There seems no doubt that *we are each and all of us to some extent victims of habit-neurosis.* We have to admit the wider potential range and the habitually narrow actual use. We live subject to arrest by degrees of fatigue which we have come only from habit to obey. Most of us may learn to push the barrier farther off, and to live in perfect comfort on much higher levels of power.

Country people and city people, as a class, illustrate this difference. The rapid rate of life, the number of decisions in an hour, the many things to keep account of, in a busy city man's or woman's life, seem monstrous to a country brother. He doesn't see how we live at all. A day in New York or Chicago fills him with terror. The danger and noise make it appear like a permanent earthquake. But *settle* him there, and in a year or two he will have caught the pulse-beat. He will vibrate to the city's rhythms; and if he only succeeds in his avocation, whatever that may be, he will find a joy in all the hurry and the tension, he will keep the pace as well as any of us, and get as much out of himself in any week as he ever did in ten weeks in the country.

The stimuli of those who successfully respond and undergo the transformation here, are duty, the example of others, and crowd-pressure and contagion. The transformation, moreover, is a chronic one: the new level of energy becomes permanent. The duties of new offices of trust are constantly producing this effect on human beings appointed to them. The physiologists call a stimulus "dynamogenic" when it increases the muscular contractions of men to whom it is applied; but appeals can be dynamogenic morally as well as muscularly. We are witnessing here in America today the dynamogenic effect of a very exalted political office upon the energies of an individual who had already manifested a healthy amount of energy before the office came.

Humbler examples show perhaps still better what chronic effects duty's appeal may produce in chosen individuals. John Stuart Mill somewhere says that women excel men in the power of keeping up sustained moral excitement. Every case of illness nursed by wife or mother is a proof of this; and where can one find greater examples of sustained endurance than in those thousands of poor homes where the woman successfully holds the family together and keeps it going by taking all the thought and doing all the work— nursing, teaching, cooking, washing, sewing, scrubbing, saving, helping neighbors, "choring" outside—where does the catalogue end? If she does a bit of scolding now and then, who can blame her? But often she does just the reverse; keeping the children clean and the man good tempered, and soothing and smoothing the whole neighborhood into finer shape.

Eighty years ago a certain Montyon left to the Académie Française a sum of money to be given in small prizes to the best examples of "virtue" of the year. The academy's committees, with great good sense, have shown a partiality to virtues simple and chronic, rather than to her spasmodic and dramatic flights; and the exemplary housewives reported on have been wonderful and admirable enough. In Paul Bourget's report for this year we find numerous cases, of which this is a type: Jeanne Chaix, eldest of six children; mother insane, father chronically ill. Jeanne, with no money but her wages at a pasteboard-box factory, directs the household, brings up the children, and successfully maintains the family of eight, which thus subsists, morally as well as materially, by the sole force of her valiant will. In some of these French cases charity to outsiders is added to the inner family burden; or helpless relatives, young or old, are adopted, as if the strength were inexhaustible and ample for every appeal. Details are too long to quote here; but human nature, responding to the call of duty, appears nowhere sublimer than in the person of these humble heroines of family life.

Turning from more chronic to acuter proofs of human nature's reserves of power, we find that the stimuli that carry us over the usually effective dam are most often the classic emotional ones, love, anger, crowd-contagion or despair. Despair lames most people, but it wakes others fully up. Every siege or shipwreck or polar expedition brings out some hero who keeps the whole company in heart. Last year there was a terrible colliery explosion at Courrières in France. Two hundred corpses, if I remember rightly, were exhumed. After twenty days of excavation the rescuers heard a voice. *"Me voici,"* said the first man unearthed. He proved to be a collier named Nemy, who had taken command of thirteen others in the darkness, disciplined them and cheered them, and brought them out alive. Hardly any of them could see or speak or walk when brought into the day. Five days later, a different type of vital endurance was unexpectedly unburied in the person of one Berton who, isolated from any but dead companions, had been able to sleep away most of his time.

A new position of responsibility will usually show a man to be a far stronger creature than was supposed. Cromwell's and Grant's careers are the stock examples of how war will wake a man up. I owe to Professor C. E. Norton, my colleague, the permission to print part of a private letter from Colonel Baird-Smith written shortly after the six weeks' siege of Delhi, in 1857, for the victorious issue of which that excellent officer was chiefly to be thanked. He writes as follows:

". . . My poor wife had some reason to think that war and disease between them had left very little of a husband to take under nursing when she got him again. An attack of camp-scurvy had filled my mouth with sores, shaken every joint in my body, and covered me all over with sores and livid spots, so that I was marvellously unlovely to look upon. A smart knock on the ankle-joint from the splinter of a shell that burst in my face, in itself a mere *bagatelle* of a wound, had been of necessity neglected under the pressing and incessant calls upon me, and had grown worse and worse till the whole foot below the ankle became a black mass and seemed to threaten mortification. I insisted, however, on being allowed to use it till the place was taken, mortification or no; and though the pain was sometimes horrible, I carried my point

and kept up to the last. On the day after the assault I had an
unlucky fall on some bad ground, and it was an open question for
a day or two whether I hadn't broken my arm at the elbow. Fortunately it turned out to be only a severe sprain, but I am still
conscious of the wrench it gave me. To crown the whole pleasant
catalogue, I was worn to a shadow by a constant diarrhœa, and
consumed as much opium as would have done credit to my father-
in-law [Thomas De Quincey]. However, thank God, I have a good
share of Tapleyism in me and come out strong under difficulties.
I think I may confidently say that no man ever saw me out of heart,
or ever heard one croaking word from me even when our prospects
were gloomiest. We were sadly scourged by the cholera, and it
was almost appalling to me to find that out of twenty-seven officers
present, I could only muster fifteen for the operations of the attack.
However, it was done, and after it was done came the collapse.
Don't be horrified when I tell you that for the whole of the actual
siege, and in truth for some little time before, I almost lived on
brandy. Appetite for food I had none, but I forced myself to eat just
sufficient to sustain life, and I had an incessant craving for brandy
as the strongest stimulant I could get. Strange to say, I was quite
unconscious of its affecting me in the slightest degree. *The excitement of the work was so great that no lesser one seemed to have
any chance against it, and I certainly never found my intellect
clearer or my nerves stronger in my life.* It was only my wretched
body that was weak, and the moment the real work was done by
our becoming complete masters of Delhi, I broke down without
delay and discovered that if I wished to live I must continue no
longer the system that had kept me up until the crisis was passed.
With it passed away as if in a moment all desire to stimulate, and
a perfect loathing of my late staff of life took possession of me."

Such experiences show how profound is the alteration in the
manner in which, under excitement, our organism will sometimes
perform its physiological work. The processes of repair become
different when the reserves have to be used, and for weeks and
months the deeper use may go on.

Morbid cases, here as elsewhere, lay the normal machinery bare.
In the first number of Dr. Morton Prince's *Journal of Abnormal
Psychology*, Dr. Janet has discussed five cases of morbid impulse,

with an explanation that is precious for my present point of view. One is a girl who eats, eats, eats, all day. Another walks, walks, walks, and gets her food from an automobile that escorts her. Another is a dipsomaniac. A fourth pulls out her hair. A fifth wounds her flesh and burns her skin. Hitherto such freaks of impulse have received Greek names (as bulimia, dromomania, etc.) and been scientifically disposed of as "episodic syndromata of hereditary degeneration." But it turns out that Janet's cases are all what he calls psychasthenics, or victims of a chronic sense of weakness, torpor, lethargy, fatigue, insufficiency, impossibility, unreality and powerlessness of will; and that in each and all of them the particular activity pursued, deleterious though it be, has the temporary result of raising the sense of vitality and making the patient feel alive again. These things reanimate: they would reanimate *us,* but it happens that in each patient the particular freak-activity chosen is the only thing that does reanimate; and therein lies the morbid state. The way to treat such persons is to discover to them more usual and useful ways of throwing their stores of vital energy into gear.

Colonel Baird-Smith, needing to draw on altogether extraordinary stores of energy, found that brandy and opium were ways of throwing them into gear.

Such cases are humanly typical. We are all to some degree oppressed, unfree. We don't come to our own. It is there, but we don't get at it. The threshold must be made to shift. Then many of us find that an eccentric activity—a "spree," say—relieves. There is no doubt that to some men sprees and excesses of almost any kind are medicinal, temporarily at any rate, in spite of what the moralists and doctors say.

But when the normal tasks and stimulations of life don't put a man's deeper levels of energy on tap, and he requires distinctly deleterious excitements, his constitution verges on the abnormal. The normal opener of deeper and deeper levels of energy is the will. The difficulty is to use it, to make the effort which the word volition implies. But if we *do* make it (or if a god, though he were only the god Chance, makes it through us), it will act dynamogenically on us for a month. It is notorious that a single successful effort of moral volition, such as saying "no" to some habitual temptation, or performing some courageous act, will launch a man on a higher level of energy for days and weeks, will give him a new range of power. "In the act of uncorking a whiskey bottle which I had brought home to get drunk upon," said a man to me, "I suddenly found myself running out into the garden, where I smashed it on the ground. I felt so happy and uplifted after this act, that for two months I wasn't tempted to touch a drop."

The emotions and excitements due to usual situations are the usual inciters of the will. But these act discontinuously; and in the intervals the shallower levels of life tend to close in and shut us off. Accordingly the best practical knowers of the human soul have invented the thing known as methodical ascetic discipline to keep the deeper levels constantly in reach. Beginning with easy tasks, passing to harder ones, and exercising day by day, it is, I believe, admitted that disciples of asceticism can reach very high levels of freedom and power of will.

Ignatius Loyola's spiritual exercises must have produced this result in innumerable devotees. But the most venerable ascetic system, and the one whose results have the most voluminous experimental corroboration, is undoubtedly the Yoga system in Hindustan. From time immemorial, by Hatha Yoga, Raja Yoga, Karma Yoga, or whatever code of practice it might be, Hindu aspirants to perfection have trained themselves, month in and out, for years. The result claimed, and certainly in many cases accorded by impartial judges, is strength of character, personal power, unshakability of soul. In an article in the *Philosophical Review*, from which I am largely copying here, I have quoted at great length the experience with "Hatha Yoga" of a very gifted European friend of mine who, by persistently carrying out for several months its methods of fasting from food and sleep, its exercises in breathing and thought-concentration, and its fantastic posture-gymnastics, seems to have succeeded in waking up deeper and deeper levels of will and moral and intellectual power in himself, and to have escaped from a decidedly menacing brain condition of the "circular" type, from which he had suffered for years.

Judging by my friend's letters, of which the last I have is written fourteen months after the Yoga training began, there can be no doubt of his relative regeneration. He has undergone material trials with indifference, travelled third-class on Mediterranean steamers, and fourth-class on African trains, living with the poorest Arabs and sharing their unaccustomed food, all with equanimity. His devotion to certain interests has been put to heavy strain, and nothing is more remarkable to me than the changed moral tone with which he reports the situation. A profound modification has unquestionably occurred in the running of his mental machinery. The gearing has changed, and his will is available otherwise than it was.

My friend is a man of very peculiar temperament. Few of us would have had the will to start upon the Yoga training, which, once started, seemed to conjure the further will-power needed out of itself. And not all of those who could launch themselves would have reached the same results. The Hindus themselves admit that in some men the results may come without call or bell. My friend writes to me: "You are quite right in thinking that religious crises, love-crises, indignation-crises may awaken in a very short time powers similar to those reached by years of patient Yoga-practice."

Probably most medical men would treat this individual's case as one of what it is fashionable now to call by the name of "self-suggestion," or "expectant attention"—as if those phrases were explanatory, or meant more than the fact that certain men can be influenced, while others cannot be influenced, by certain sorts of *ideas*. This leads me to say a word about ideas considered as dynamogenic agents, or stimuli for unlocking what would otherwise be unused reservoirs of individual power.

One thing that ideas do is to contradict other ideas and keep us from believing them. An idea that thus negates a first idea may itself in turn be negated by a third idea, and the first idea may thus regain its natural influence over our belief and determine our behavior. Our philosophic and religious development proceeds thus by credulities, negations, and the negating of negations.

But whether for arousing or for stopping belief, ideas may fail to be efficacious, just as a wire at one time alive with electricity may at another time be dead. Here our insight into causes fails us, and we can only note results in general terms. In general, whether a given idea shall be a live idea depends more on the person into whose mind it is injected than on the idea itself. Which is the suggestive idea for this person, and which for that one? Mr. Fletcher's disciples regenerate themselves by the idea (and the fact) that they are chewing, and re-chewing, and super-chewing their food. Dr. Dewey's pupils regenerate themselves by going without their breakfast—a fact, but also an ascetic idea. Not everyone can use *these* ideas with the same success.

But apart from such individually varying susceptibilities, there are common lines along which men simply as men tend to be inflammable by ideas. As certain objects naturally awaken love, anger, or cupidity, so certain ideas naturally awaken the energies of loyalty, courage, endurance, or devotion. When these ideas are effective in an individual's life, their effect is often very great indeed. They may transfigure it, unlocking innumerable powers which, but for the idea, would never have come into play. "Fatherland," "the Flag," "the Union," "Holy Church," "the Monroe Doctrine," "Truth," "Science," "Liberty," Garibaldi's phrase, "Rome or Death," etc., are so many examples of energy-releasing ideas. The social nature of such phrases is an essential factor of their dynamic power. They are forces of detent in situations in which no other force produces equivalent effects, and each is a force of detent only in a specific group of men.

The memory that an oath or vow has been made will nerve one to abstinences and efforts otherwise impossible; witness the "pledge" in the history of the temperance movement. A mere promise to his sweetheart will clean up a youth's life all over—at any rate for a time. For such effects an educated susceptibility is required. The idea of one's "honor," for example, unlocks energy only in those of us who have had the education of a "gentleman," so called.

That delightful being, Prince Pueckler-Muskau, writes to his wife from England that he has invented "a sort of artificial resolution respecting things that are difficult of performance. My device," he continues, "is this: *I give my word of honor most solemnly to myself* to do or to leave undone this or that. I am of course extremely cautious in the use of this expedient, but when once the word is given, even though I afterwards think I have been precipitate or mistaken, I hold it to be perfectly irrevocable, whatever

inconveniences I foresee likely to result. If I were capable of breaking my word after such mature consideration, I should lose all
respect for myself,—and what man of sense would not prefer death
to such an alternative? . . . When the mysterious formula is pronounced, no alteration in my own view, nothing short of physical
impossibilities, must, for the welfare of my soul, alter my will. . . .
I find something very satisfactory in the thought that man has the
power of framing such props and weapons out of the most trivial
materials, indeed out of nothing, merely by the force of his will,
which thereby truly deserves the name of omnipotent."

Conversions, whether they be political, scientific, philosophic, or
religious, form another way in which bound energies are let loose.
They unify us, and put a stop to ancient mental interferences. The
result is freedom, and often a great enlargement of power. A belief
that thus settles upon an individual always acts as a challenge to
his will. But, for the particular challenge to operate, he must be
the right challeng*ee*. In religious conversions we have so fine an
adjustment that the idea may be in the mind of the challengee for
years before it exerts effects; and why it should do so then is
often so far from obvious that the event is taken for a miracle of
grace, and not a natural occurrence. Whatever it is, it may be a
highwater mark of energy, in which "noes," once impossible, are
easy, and in which a new range of "yeses" gains the right of way.

We are just now witnessing a very copious unlocking of energies
by ideas in the persons of those converts to "New Thought,"
"Christian Science," "Metaphysical Healing," or other forms of
spiritual philosophy, who are so numerous among us today. The
ideas here are healthy-minded and optimistic; and it is quite obvious that a wave of religious activity, analogous in some respects
to the spread of early Christianity, Buddhism, and Moham-
medanism, is passing over our American world. The common
feature of these optimistic faiths is that they all tend to the suppression of what Mr. Horace Fletcher calls "fearthought." Fearthought
he defines as the "self-suggestion of inferiority"; so that one may
say that these systems all operate by the suggestion of power. And
the power, small or great, comes in various shapes to the individual,—power, as he will tell you, not to "mind" things that used to

vex him, power to concentrate his mind, good cheer, good temper —in short, to put it mildly, a firmer, more elastic moral tone.

The most genuinely saintly person I have ever known is a friend of mine now suffering from cancer of the breast—I hope that she may pardon my citing her here as an example of what ideas can do. Her ideas have kept her a practically well woman for months after she should have given up and gone to bed. They have annuled all pain and weakness and given her a cheerful active life, unusually beneficent to others to whom she has afforded help. Her doctors, acquiescing in results they could not understand, have had the good sense to let her go her own way.

How far the mind-cure movement is destined to extend its influence, or what intellectual modifications it may yet undergo, no one can foretell. It is essentially a religious movement, and to academically nurtured minds its utterances are tasteless and often grotesque enough. It also incurs the natural enmity of medical politicians, and of the whole trades-union wing of that profession. But no unprejudiced observer can fail to recognize its importance as a social phenomenon today, and the higher medical minds are already trying to interpret it fairly, and make its power available for their own therapeutic ends.

Dr. Thomas Hyslop, of the great West Riding Asylum in England, said last year to the British Medical Association that the best sleep-producing agent which his practice had revealed to him was *prayer*. I say this, he added (I am sorry here that I must quote from memory), purely as a medical man. The exercise of prayer, in those who habitually exert it, must be regarded by us doctors as the most adequate and normal of all the pacifiers of the mind and calmers of the nerves.

But in few of us are functions not tied up by the exercise of other functions. Relatively few medical men and scientific men, I fancy, can pray. Few can carry on any living commerce with "God." Yet many of us are well aware of how much freer and abler our lives would be, were such important forms of energizing not sealed up by the critical atmosphere in which we have been reared. There are in every one potential forms of activity that actually are shunted out from use. Part of the imperfect vitality under which we labor can thus be easily explained. One part of our mind dams up—even *damns* up!—the other parts.

Conscience makes cowards of us all. Social conventions prevent us from telling the truth after the fashion of the heroes and heroines of Bernard Shaw. We all know persons who are models of excellence, but who belong to the extreme philistine type of mind. So deadly is their intellectual respectability that we can't converse about certain subjects at all, can't let our minds play over them, can't even mention them in their presence. I have numbered among my dearest friends persons thus inhibited intellectually, with whom I would gladly have been able to talk freely about certain interests of mine, certain authors, say, as Bernard Shaw, Chesterton, Edward Carpenter, H. G. Wells, but it wouldn't do, it made them too uncomfortable, they wouldn't play, I had to be silent. An intellect thus tied down by literality and decorum makes on one the same sort of an impression that an able-bodied man would who should habituate himself to do his work with only one of his fingers, locking up the rest of his organism and leaving it unused.

I trust that by this time I have said enough to convince the reader both of the truth and of the importance of my thesis. The two questions, first, that of the possible extent of our powers; and, second, that of the various avenues of approach to them, the various keys for unlocking them in diverse individuals, dominate the whole problem of individual and national education. We need a topography of the limits of human power, similar to the chart which oculists use of the field of human vision. We need also a study of the various types of human being with reference to the different ways in which their energy-reserves may be appealed to and set loose. Biographies and individual experiences of every kind may be drawn upon for evidence here.

The School and Social Progress

JOHN DEWEY

John Dewey was born in Burlington, Vermont, in 1859, and did his undergraduate work at the University of Vermont. In 1884 he was granted a doctorate by the recently instituted graduate school of Johns Hopkins. After a decade of teaching philosophy at the Universities of Michigan and Minnesota, he went to the new University of Chicago in 1894 as chairman of the department of philosophy, psychology, and pedagogy. This essay was the first of three lectures given in 1899 to an audience of parents and others interested in the university's elementary school and published in Dewey's *The School and Society* (University of Chicago Press, 1900). His other major works include *Ethics,* with J. H. Tufts (1908); *Reconstruction in Philosophy* (1920); *Human Nature and Conduct* (1922); *Art as Experience* (1934); and *Logic: The Theory of Inquiry* (1938). From 1904 until his retirement, Dewey was professor of philosophy at Columbia. He died in 1952.

WE ARE APT to look at the school from an individualistic standpoint, as something between teacher and pupil, or between teacher and parent. That which interests us most is naturally the progress made by the individual child of our acquaintance, his normal physical development, his advance in ability to read, write, and figure, his growth in the knowledge of geography and history, improvement in manners, habits of promptness, order, and industry —it is from such standards as these that we judge the work of the school. And rightly so. Yet the range of the outlook needs to be enlarged. What the best and wisest parent wants for his own child,

17

that must the community want for all of its children. Any other ideal for our schools is narrow and unlovely; acted upon, it destroys our democracy. All that society has accomplished for itself is put, through the agency of the school, at the disposal of its future members. All its better thoughts of itself it hopes to realize through the new possibilities thus opened to its future self. Here individualism and socialism are at one. Only by being true to the full growth of all the individuals who make it up, can society by any chance be true to itself. And in the self-direction thus given, nothing counts as much as the school, for, as Horace Mann said, "Where anything is growing, one former is worth a thousand re-formers."

Whenever we have in mind the discussion of a new movement in education, it is especially necessary to take the broader, or social view. Otherwise, changes in the school institution and tradition will be looked at as the arbitrary inventions of particular teachers, at the worst transitory fads, and at the best merely improvements in certain details—and this is the plane upon which it is too customary to consider school changes. It is as rational to conceive of the locomotive or the telegraph as personal devices. The modification going on in the method and curriculum of education is as much a product of the changed social situation, and as much an effort to meet the needs of the new society that is forming, as are changes in modes of industry and commerce.

It is to this, then, that I especially ask your attention: the effort to conceive what roughly may be termed the "New Education" in the light of larger changes in society. Can we connect this "New Education" with the general march of events? If we can, it will lose its isolated character, and will cease to be an affair which proceeds only from the over-ingenious minds of pedagogues dealing with particular pupils. It will appear as part and parcel of the whole social evolution, and, in its more general features at least, as inevitable. Let us then ask after the main aspects of the social movement; and afterwards turn to the school to find what witness it gives of effort to put itself in line. And since it is quite impossible to cover the whole ground, I shall for the most part confine myself in this chapter to one typical thing in the modern school movement— that which passes under the name of manual training—hoping if the relation of that to changed social conditions appears, we shall be ready to concede the point as well regarding other educational innovations.

I make no apology for not dwelling at length upon the social changes in question. Those I shall mention are writ so large that he who runs may read. The change that comes first to mind, the one that overshadows and even controls all others, is the industrial one—the application of science resulting in the great inventions that have utilized the forces of nature on a vast and inexpensive scale: the growth of a world-wide market as the object of production, of vast manufacturing centers to supply this market, of cheap and rapid means of communication and distribution between all its parts. Even as to its feebler beginnings, this change is not much more than a century old; in many of its most important aspects it falls within the short span of those now living. One can hardly believe there has been a revolution in all history so rapid, so extensive, so complete. Through it the face of the earth is making over, even as to its physical forms; political boundaries are wiped out and moved about, as if they were indeed only lines on a paper map; population is hurriedly gathered into cities from the ends of the earth; habits of living are altered with startling abruptness and thoroughness; the search for the truths of nature is infinitely stimulated and facilitated, and their application to life made not only practicable, but commercially necessary. Even our moral and religious ideas and interests, the most conservative because the deepest-lying things in our nature, are profoundly affected. That this revolution should not affect education in other than formal and superficial fashion is inconceivable.

Back of the factory system lies the household and neighborhood system. Those of us who are here today need go back only one, two, or at most three generations, to find a time when the household was practically the center in which were carried on, or about which were clustered, all the typical forms of industrial occupation. The clothing worn was for the most part made in the house; the members of the household were usually familiar also with the shearing of the sheep, the carding and spinning of the wool, and the plying of the loom. Instead of pressing a button and flooding the house with electric light, the whole process of getting illumination was followed in its toilsome length from the killing of the animal and the trying of fat, to the making of wicks and dipping of candles. The supply of flour, of lumber, of foods, of building materials, of household furniture, even of metal ware, of nails, hinges, hammers, etc., was produced in the immediate neighborhood, in shops which were constantly open to inspection and often centers of neighborhood congregation. The entire industrial process stood revealed, from the production on the farm of the raw materials, till the finished article was actually put to use. Not only this, but practically every member of the household had his own share in the work. The children, as they gained in strength and capacity, were gradually initiated into the mysteries of the several processes. It was a matter of immediate and personal concern, even to the point of actual participation.

We cannot overlook the factors of discipline and of character-building involved in this: training in habits of order and of industry, and in the idea of responsibility, of obligation to do something, to produce something, in the world. There was always something which really needed to be done, and a real necessity that each member of the household should do his own part faithfully and in cooperation with others. Personalities which became effective in action were bred and tested in the medium of action. Again, we cannot overlook the importance for educational purposes of the close and intimate acquaintance got with nature at first hand, with real things and materials, with the actual processes of their manipulation, and the knowledge of their social necessities and uses. In all this there was continual training of observation, of ingenuity, constructive imagination, of logical thought, and of the sense of reality acquired through first-hand contact with actualities. The educative forces of the domestic spinning and weaving, of the sawmill, the gristmill, the cooper shop, and the blacksmith forge, were continuously operative.

No number of object-lessons, got up as object-lessons for the sake of giving information, can afford even the shadow of a substitute for acquaintance with the plants and animals of the farm and garden acquired through actual living among them and caring for them. No training of sense-organs in school, introduced for the sake of training, can begin to compete with the alertness and fulness of sense-life that comes through daily intimacy and interest in familiar occupations. Verbal memory can be trained in committing tasks, a certain discipline of the reasoning powers can be acquired through lessons in science and mathematics; but, after all, this is somewhat remote and shadowy compared with the training of attention and of judgment that is acquired in having to do things with a real motive behind and a real outcome ahead. At present, concentration of industry and division of labor have practically eliminated household and neighborhood occupations—at least for educational purposes. But it is useless to bemoan the departure of the good old days of children's modesty, reverence, and implicit obedience, if we expect merely by bemoaning and by exhortation to bring them back. It is radical conditions which have changed, and only an equally radical change in education suffices. We must recognize our compensations—the increase in toleration, in breadth of social judgment, the larger acquaintance with human nature, the sharpened alertness in reading signs of character and interpreting social situations, greater accuracy of adaptation to differing personalities, contact with greater commercial activities. These considerations mean much to the city-bred child of today. Yet there is a real problem: how shall we retain these advantages, and yet introduce into the school something representing the other side of life—occupations which exact personal responsibilities and which train the child with relation to the physical realities of life?

When we turn to the school, we find that one of the most striking tendencies at present is toward the introduction of so-called manual training, shop-work, and the household arts—sewing and cooking.

This has not been done "on purpose," with a full consciousness that the school must now supply that factor of training formerly taken care of in the home, but rather by instinct, by experimenting and finding that such work takes a vital hold of pupils and gives them something which was not to be got in any other way. Consciousness of its real import is still so weak that the work is often done in a half-hearted, confused, and unrelated way. The reasons assigned to justify it are painfully inadequate or sometimes even positively wrong.

If we were to cross-examine even those who are most favorably disposed to the introduction of this work into our school system, we should, I imagine, generally find the main reasons to be that such work engages the full spontaneous interest and attention of the children. It keeps them alert and active, instead of passive and receptive; it makes them more useful, more capable, and hence more inclined to be helpful at home; it prepares them to some extent for the practical duties of later life—the girls to be more efficient house managers, if not actually cooks and semp-stresses; the boys (were our educational system only adequately rounded out into trade schools) for their future vocations. I do not underestimate the worth of these reasons. Of those indicated by the changed attitude of the children I shall indeed have some-thing to say in my next talk, when speaking directly of the rela-tionship of the school to the child. But the point of view is, upon the whole, unnecessarily narrow. We must conceive of work in wood and metal, of weaving, sewing, and cooking, as methods of life, not as distinct studies.

We must conceive of them in their social significance, as types of the processes by which society keeps itself going, as agencies for bringing home to the child some of the primal necessities of community life, and as ways in which these needs have been met by the growing insight and ingenuity of man; in short, as instru-mentalities through which the school itself shall be made a genuine form of active community life, instead of a place set apart in which to learn lessons.

A society is a number of people held together because they are working along common lines, in a common spirit, and with refer-ence to common aims. The common needs and aims demand a growing interchange of thought and growing unity of sympathetic feeling. The radical reason that the present school cannot organize itself as a natural social unit is because just this element of com-mon and productive activity is absent. Upon the playground, in game and sport, social organization takes place spontaneously and inevitably. There is something to do, some activity to be carried on, requiring natural divisions of labor, selection of leaders and fol-lowers, mutual cooperation and emulation. In the schoolroom the motive and the cement of social organization are alike wanting. Upon the ethical side, the tragic weakness of the present school is that it endeavors to prepare future members of the social order in a medium in which the conditions of the social spirit are eminently wanting.

The difference that appears when occupations are made the articulating centers of school life is not easy to describe in words; it is a difference in motive, of spirit and atmosphere. As one enters a busy kitchen in which a group of children are actively engaged in the preparation of food, the psychological difference, the change from more or less passive and inert recipiency and restraint to one of buoyant outgoing energy, is so obvious as fairly to strike one in the face. Indeed, to those whose image of the school is rigidly set the change is sure to give a shock. But the change in the social attitude is equally marked. The mere absorbing of facts and truths is so exclusively individual an affair that it tends very naturally to pass into selfishness. There is no obvious social motive for the acquirement of mere learning; there is no clear social gain in success thereat. Indeed, almost the only measure for success is a competitive one, in the bad sense of that term —a comparison of results in the recitation or in the examination to see which child has succeeded in getting ahead of others in storing up, in accumulating the maximum of information. So thoroughly is this the prevailing atmosphere that for one child to help another in his task has become a school crime. Where the school work consists in simply learning lessons, mutual assistance, instead of being the most natural form of cooperation and association, becomes a clandestine effort to relieve one's neighbor of his proper duties. Where active work is going on all this is changed. Helping others, instead of being a form of charity which impoverishes the recipient, is simply an aid in setting free the powers and furthering the impulse of the one helped. A spirit of free communication, of interchange of ideas, suggestions, results, both successes and failures of previous experiences, becomes the dominating note of the recitation. So far as emulation enters in, it is in the comparison of individuals, not with regard to the quantity of information personally absorbed, but with reference to the quality of work done— the genuine community standard of value. In an informal but all the more pervasive way, the school life organizes itself on a social basis.

Within this organization is found the principle of school discipline or order. Of course, order is simply a thing which is relative to an end. If you have the end in view of forty or fifty children learning certain set lessons, to be recited to a teacher, your discipline must be devoted to securing that result. But if the end in view is the development of a spirit of social cooperation and community life, discipline must grow out of and be relative to this. There is little of one sort of order where things are in process of construction; there is a certain disorder in any busy workshop; there is not silence; persons are not engaged in maintaining certain fixed physical postures; their arms are not folded; they are not holding their books thus and so. They are doing a variety of things, and there is the confusion, the bustle, that results from activity. But out of occupation, out of doing things that are to produce results, and out of doing these in a social and cooperative way, there is born a discipline of its own kind and type. Our whole conception of school discipline changes when we get this point of view. In critical moments we all realize that the only discipline that stands by us, the only training that becomes intuition, is that got through life itself. That we learn from experience, and from books or the sayings of others *only* as they are related to experience, are not mere phrases. But the school has been so set apart, so isolated from the ordinary conditions and motives of life, that the place where children are sent for discipline is the one place in the world where it is most difficult to get experience—the mother of all discipline worth the name. It is only where a narrow and fixed image of traditional school discipline dominates, that one is in any danger of overlooking that deeper and infinitely wider discipline that comes from having a part to do in constructive work, in contributing to a result which, social in spirit, is none the less obvious and tangible in form—and hence in a form with reference to which responsibility may be exacted and accurate judgment passed.

The great thing to keep in mind, then, regarding the introduction into the school of various forms of active occupation, is that through them the entire spirit of the school is renewed. It has a chance to affiliate itself with life, to become the child's habitat, where he learns through directed living; instead of being only a place to learn lessons having an abstract and remote reference to some possible living to be done in the future. It gets a chance to be a miniature community, an embryonic society. This is the fundamental fact, and from this arise continuous and orderly sources of instruction. Under the industrial *régime* described, the child, after all, shared in the work, not for the sake of the sharing, but for the sake of the product. The educational results secured were real, yet incidental and dependent. But in the school the typical occupations followed are freed from all economic stress. The aim is not the economic value of the products, but the development of social power and insight. It is this liberation from narrow utilities, this openness to the possibilities of the human spirit that makes these practical activities in the school allies of art and centers of science and history.

The unity of all the sciences is found in geography. The significance of geography is that it presents the earth as the enduring home of the occupations of man. The world without its relationship to human activity is less than a world. Human industry and achievement, apart from their roots in the earth, are not even a sentiment, hardly a name. The earth is the final source of all man's food. It is his continual shelter and protection, the raw material of all his activities, and the home to whose humanizing and idealizing all his achievement returns. It is the great field, the great mine, the great source of the energies of heat, light, and electricity; the great scene of ocean, stream, mountain, and plain, of which all our agriculture and mining and lumbering, all our manufacturing and distributing agencies, are but the partial elements and factors. It is through occupations determined by this environment that mankind has made its historical and political progress. It is through these occupations that the intellectual and emotional interpretation of nature has been developed. It is through what we do in and with the world that we read its meaning and measure its value.

In educational terms, this means that these occupations in the school shall not be mere practical devices or modes of routine employment, the gaining of better technical skill as cooks, sempstresses, or carpenters, but active centers of scientific insight into natural materials and processes, points of departure whence children shall be led out into a realization of the historic development of man. The actual significance of this can be told better through one illustration taken from actual school work than by general discourse.

There is nothing which strikes more oddly upon the average intelligent visitor than to see boys as well as girls of ten, twelve, and thirteen years of age engaged in sewing and weaving. If we look at this from the standpoint of preparation of the boys for sewing on buttons and making patches, we get a narrow and utilitarian conception—a basis that hardly justifies giving prominence to this sort of work in the school. But if we look at it from another side, we find that this work gives the point of departure from which the child can trace and follow the progress of mankind in history, getting an insight also into the materials used and the mechanical principles involved. In connection with these occupations, the historic development of man is recapitulated. For example, the children are first given the raw material—the flax, the cotton plant, the wool as it comes from the back of the sheep (if we could take them to the place where the sheep are sheared, so much the better). Then a study is made of these materials from the standpoint of their adaptation to the uses to which they may be put. For instance, a comparison of the cotton fiber with wool fiber is made. I did not know, until the children told me, that the reason for the late development of the cotton industry as compared with the woolen is that the cotton fiber is so very difficult to free by hand from the seeds. The children in one group worked thirty minutes freeing cotton fibers from the boll and seeds, and succeeded in getting out less than one ounce. They could easily believe that one person could gin only one pound a day by hand, and could understand why their ancestors wore woolen instead of cotton clothing. Among other things discovered as affecting their relative utilities, was the shortness of the cotton fiber as compared with that of wool, the former being one-tenth of an inch in length, while that of the latter is an inch in length; also that the fibers of cotton are smooth and do not cling together, while the wool has a certain roughness which makes the fibers stick, thus assisting the spinning. The children worked this out for themselves with the actual material, aided by questions and suggestions from the teacher.

They then followed the processes necessary for working the

fibers up into cloth. They reinvented the first frame for carding the wool—a couple of boards with sharp pins in them for scratching it out. They redevised the simplest process for spinning the wool—a pierced stone or some other weight through which the wool is passed, and which as it is twirled draws out the fiber; next the top, which was spun on the floor, while the children kept the wool in their hands until it was gradually drawn out and wound upon it. Then the children are introduced to the invention next in historic order, working it out experimentally, thus seeing its necessity, and tracing its effects, not only upon that particular industry, but upon modes of social life—in this way passing in review the entire process up to the present complete loom, and all that goes with the application of science in the use of our present available powers. I need not speak of the science involved in this— the study of the fibers, of geographical features, the conditions under which raw materials are grown, the great centers of manufacture and distribution, the physics involved in the machinery of production; nor, again, of the historical side—the influence which these inventions have had upon humanity. You can concentrate the history of all mankind into the evolution of the flax, cotton, and wool fibers into clothing. I do not mean that this is the only, or the best, center. But it is true that certain very real and important avenues to the consideration of the history of the race are thus opened—that the mind is introduced to much more fundamental and controlling influences than usually appear in the political and chronological records that pass for history.

Now, what is true of this one instance of fibers used in fabrics (and, of course, I have only spoken of one or two elementary phases of that) is true in its measure of every material used in every occupation, and of the processes employed. The occupation supplies the child with a genuine motive; it gives him experience at first hand; it brings him into contact with realities. It does all this, but in addition it is liberalized throughout by translation into its historic values and scientific equivalencies. With the growth of the child's mind in power and knowledge it ceases to be a pleasant occupation merely, and becomes more and more a medium, an instrument, an organ,—and is thereby transformed.

This, in turn, has its bearing upon the teaching of science. Under present conditions, all activity, to be successful, has to be directed somewhere and somehow by the scientific expert—it is a case of applied science. This connection should determine its place in education. It is not only that the occupations, the so-called manual or industrial work in the school, give the opportunity for the introduction of science which illuminates them, which makes them material, freighted with meaning, instead of being mere devices of hand and eye; but that the scientific insight thus gained becomes an indispensable instrument of free and active participation in modern social life. Plato somewhere speaks of the slave as one who in his actions does not express his own ideas, but those of some other man. It is our social problem now, even more urgent than in the time of Plato, that method, purpose, understanding, shall exist in the consciousness of the one who does the work, that his activity shall have meaning to himself.

When occupations in the school are conceived in this broad and generous way, I can only stand lost in wonder at the objections so often heard that such occupations are out of place in the school because they are materialistic, utilitarian, or even menial in their tendency. It sometimes seems to me that those who make these objections must live in quite another world. The world in which most of us live is a world in which everyone has a calling and occupation, something to do. Some are managers and others are subordinates. But the great thing for one as for the other is that each shall have had the education which enables him to see within his daily work all there is in it of large and human significance. How many of the employed are today mere appendages to the machines which they operate! This may be due in part to the machine itself, or to the *régime* which lays so much stress upon the products of the machine; but it is certainly due in large part to the fact that the worker has had no opportunity to develop his imagination and his sympathetic insight as to the social and scientific values found in his work. At present, the impulses which lie at the basis of the industrial system are either practically neglected or positively distorted during the school period. Until the instincts of construction and production are systematically laid hold of in the years of childhood and youth, until they are trained in social directions, enriched by historical interpretation, controlled and illuminated by scientific methods, we certainly are in no position even to locate the source of our economic evils, much less to deal with them effectively.

If we go back a few centuries, we find a practical monopoly of learning. The term *possession* of learning was, indeed, a happy one. Learning was a class matter. This was a necessary result of social conditions. There were not in existence any means by which the multitude could possibly have access to intellectual resources. These were stored up and hidden away in manuscripts. Of these there were at best only a few, and it required long and toilsome preparation to be able to do anything with them. A high-priest-hood of learning, which guarded the treasury of truth and which doled it out to the masses under severe restrictions, was the inevitable expression of these conditions. But, as a direct result of the industrial revolution of which we have been speaking, this has been changed. Printing was invented; it was made commercial. Books, magazines, papers were multiplied and cheapened. As a result of the locomotive and telegraph, frequent, rapid, and cheap intercommunication by mails and electricity was called into being. Travel has been rendered easy; freedom of movement, with its accompanying exchange of ideas, indefinitely facilitated. The result has been an intellectual revolution. Learning has been put into circulation. While there still is, and probably always will be, a particular class having the special business of inquiry in hand, a distinctively learned class is henceforth out of the question. It is an anachronism. Knowledge is no longer an immobile solid; it has been liquefied. It is actively moving in all the currents of society itself.

It is easy to see that this revolution, as regards the materials of knowledge, carries with it a marked change in the attitude of the individual. Stimuli of an intellectual sort pour in upon us in all kinds of ways. The merely intellectual life, the life of scholarship and of learning, thus gets a very altered value. Academic and scholastic, instead of being titles of honor, are becoming terms of reproach.

But all this means a necessary change in the attitude of the school, one of which we are as yet far from realizing the full force.

Our school methods, and to a very considerable extent our curriculum, are inherited from the period when learning and command of certain symbols, affording as they did the only access to learning, were all-important. The ideals of this period are still largely in control, even where the outward methods and studies have been changed. We sometimes hear the introduction of manual training, art and science into the elementary, and even the secondary schools, deprecated on the ground that they tend toward the production of specialists—that they detract from our present scheme of generous, liberal culture. The point of this objection would be ludicrous if it were not often so effective as to make it tragic. It is our present education which is highly specialized, one-sided and narrow. It is an education dominated almost entirely by the mediaeval conception of learning. It is something which appeals for the most part simply to the intellectual aspect of our natures, our desire to learn, to accumulate information, and to get control of the symbols of learning; not to our impulses and tendencies to make, to do, to create, to produce, whether in the form of utility or of art. The very fact that manual training, art and science are objected to as technical, as tending toward mere specialism, is of itself as good testimony as could be offered to the specialized aim which controls current education. Unless education had been virtually identified with the exclusively intellectual pursuits, with learning as such, all these materials and methods would be welcome, would be greeted with the utmost hospitality.

While training for the profession of learning is regarded as the type of culture, or a liberal education, that of a mechanic, a musician, a lawyer, a doctor, a farmer, a merchant, or a railroad manager is regarded as purely technical and professional. The result is that which we see about us everywhere—the division into "cultured" people and "workers," the separation of theory and practice. Hardly one per cent of the entire school population ever attains to what we call higher education; only five per cent to the grade of our high school; while much more than half leave on or before the completion of the fifth year of the elementary grade. The simple facts of the case are that in the great majority of human beings the distinctively intellectual interest is not dominant. They have the so-called practical impulse and disposition. In many of those in whom by nature intellectual interest is strong, social conditions prevent its adequate realization. Consequently by far the larger number of pupils leave school as soon as they have acquired the rudiments of learning, as soon as they have enough of the symbols of reading, writing, and calculating to be of practical use to them in getting a living. While our educational leaders are talking of culture, the development of personality, etc., as the end and aim of education, the great majority of those who pass under the tuition of the school regard it only as a narrowly practical tool with which to get bread and butter enough to eke out a restricted life. If we were to conceive our educational end and aim in a less exclusive way, if we were to introduce into educational processes the activities which appeal to those whose dominant interest is to do and to make, we should find the hold of the school upon its members to be more vital, more prolonged, containing more of culture.

But why should I make this labored presentation? The obvious fact is that our social life has undergone a thorough and radical change. If our education is to have any meaning for life, it must pass through an equally complete transformation. This transformation is not something to appear suddenly, to be executed in a day by conscious purpose. It is already in progress. Those modifications of our school system which often appear (even to those most actively concerned with them, to say nothing of their spectators) to be mere changes of detail, mere improvement within the school mechanism, are in reality signs and evidences of evolution. The introduction of active occupations, of nature study, of elementary science, of art, of history; the relegation of the merely symbolic and formal to a secondary position; the change in the moral school atmosphere, in the relation of pupils and teachers— of discipline; the introduction of more active, expressive, and self-directing factors—all these are not mere accidents, they are necessities of the larger social evolution. It remains but to organize all these factors, to appreciate them in their fullness of meaning, and to put the ideas and ideals involved into complete, uncompromising possession of our school system. To do this means to make each one of our schools an embryonic community life, active with types of occupations that reflect the life of the larger society, and permeated throughout with the spirit of art, history, and science. When the school introduces and trains each child of society into membership within such a little community, saturating him with the spirit of service, and providing him with the instruments of effective self-direction, we shall have the deepest and best guaranty of a larger society which is worthy, lovely, and harmonious.

The Intellectual Pre-eminence
of Jews in Modern Europe

THORSTEIN VEBLEN

Thorstein Veblen (1857–1929) was born in Wisconsin near Lake
Michigan, one of twelve children of a Norwegian immigrant farmer.
Many of his most incisive comments depend on his continuing
estrangement from American customs and values, and—although he
is widely regarded today as our greatest social scientist—his academic
career was marked by repeated frustrations and occasional small
successes. After studying at Carleton College and at Johns Hopkins,
he was granted a Ph.D. in philosophy by Yale in 1884. Even so,
he could not get a teaching position and spent seven years as a farmer
in Minnesota. He re-entered academic life at Cornell, and then
became an instructor in economics at Chicago. He went next to
Stanford. Forced to leave because of difficulties involving a woman,
he taught at Missouri from 1911 to 1918. He taught a while after
the war at the New School for Social Research in New York, and
his life petered out. This essay was first published in the *Political
Science Quarterly,* XXXIV (1919) and reprinted in the posthumous
Essays in Our Changing Order, edited by Leon Ardzrooni (New
York: Viking, 1934). It also appeared in *The Portable Veblen,* edited
by Max Lerner, copyright 1934, 1938 by The Viking Press, Inc., and
is reprinted with their permission.

AMONG ALL the clamorous projects of national self-determination
which surround the return of peace the proposal of the Zionists
is notable for sobriety, good will and a poise of self-assurance.
More confidently and perspicuously than all the others, the Zionists

propose a rehabilitation of their national integrity under a régime of live and let live, "with charity for all, with malice toward none." Yet it is always a project for withdrawal upon themselves, a scheme of national demarcation between Jew and gentile; indeed, it is a scheme of territorial demarcation and national frontiers of the conventional sort, within which Jews and Jewish traits, traditions and aspirations are to find scope and breathing space for a home-bred culture and a free unfolding of all that is best and most characteristic in the endowment of the race. There runs through it all a dominant bias of isolation and in-breeding, and a confident persuasion that this isolation and in-breeding will bring great and good results for all concerned. The Zionists aspire to bring to full fruition all that massive endowment of spiritual and intellectual capacities of which their people have given evidence throughout their troubled history, and not least during these concluding centuries of their exile.

The whole project has an idyllic and engaging air. And any disinterested bystander will be greatly moved to wish them godspeed. Yet there comes in a regret that this experiment in isolation and in-breeding could not have been put to the test at an earlier date, before the new order of large-scale industry and universal intercourse had made any conclusive degree of such national isolation impracticable, before this same new order had so shaped the run of things that any nation or community drawn on this small scale would necessarily be dependent on and subsidiary to the run of things at large. It is now, unhappily, true that any "nation" of the size and geographical emplacement of the projected Zion will, for the present and the calculable future, necessarily be something of a national make-believe. The current state of the industrial arts will necessarily deny it a rounded and self-balanced national integrity in any substantial sense. The days of Solomon and the caravan trade which underlay the glory of Solomon are long past.

Yet much can doubtless be done by taking thought and making the most of that spirit of stubborn clannishness which has never been the least among the traits of this people. But again, to any disinterested bystander there will come the question: What is the use of it all? It is not so much a question of what is aimed at, as of the chances of its working out. The logic of the Zionist project plainly runs to the effect that, whereas this people have achieved great things while living under conditions of great adversity, scattered piecemeal among the gentiles of Europe, they are due to achieve much greater things and to reach an unexampled prosperity so soon as they shall have a chance to follow their own devices untroubled within the shelter of their own frontiers. But the doubt presents itself that the conditioning circumstances are not the same or of the same kind in the occidental twentieth century A.D. as in the oriental twelfth century B.C.; nor need it follow that those things which scattered Jews have achieved during their dispersion among the gentiles of Europe are a safe index of what things may be expected of a nation of Jews turned in upon themselves within the insulating frontiers of the Holy Land. It is on this latter point that a question is raised here as to the nature and causes of Jewish achievement in gentile Europe; and the contrast of the conditions offered by the projected Zion will present itself without argument.

It is a fact which must strike any dispassionate observer that the Jewish people have contributed much more than an even share to the intellectual life of modern Europe. So also it is plain that the civilization of Christendom continues today to draw heavily on the Jews for men devoted to science and scholarly pursuits. It is not only that men of Jewish extraction continue to supply more than a proportionate quota to the rank and file engaged in scientific and scholarly work, but a disproportionate number of the men to whom modern science and scholarship look for guidance and leadership are of the same derivation. Particularly is this true of the modern sciences, and it applies perhaps especially in the field of scientific theory, even beyond the extent of its application in the domain of workday detail. So much is notorious.

This notable and indeed highly creditable showing has, of course, not escaped the attention of those men of Jewish race who interest themselves in the fortunes of their own people. Not unusually it is set down as a national trait, as evidence of a peculiarly fortunate intellectual endowment, native and hereditary, in the Jewish people. There is much to be said for such a view, but it should not follow that any inquiry into the place and value of the Jewish people in western civilization should come to rest with this broad assertion of pre-eminence in point of native endowment.

It is true that the history of the Chosen People, late and early, throws them into a position of distinction among the nations with which they have been associated; and it will commonly be accepted without much argument that they have, both late and early, shown distinctive traits of temperament and aptitude, such as to mark them off more or less sharply from all the gentiles among whom it has been their lot to be thrown. So general is the recognition of special Jewish traits, of character and of capacity, that any refusal to recognize something which may be called a Jewish type of hereditary endowment would come to nothing much better than a borrowing of trouble.

That there should be such a tenacious spiritual and intellectual heritage transmissible within the Jewish community and marking that people off in any perceptible degree from their gentile neighbors is all the more notable in view of the known life-history of the Children of Israel. No unbiassed ethnologist will question the fact that the Jewish people are a nation of hybrids; that gentile blood of many kinds has been infused into the people in large proportions in the course of time. Indeed, none of the peoples of Christendom has been more unremittingly exposed to hybridization, in spite of all the stiff conventional precautions that have been taken to keep the breed pure. It is not a question of a surreptitious hybrid strain, such as would show itself in sporadic reversions to an alien type; but rather it is a question whether the Jewish strain itself, racially speaking, can at all reasonably be held to account for one half of the pedigree of the Jewish nation as it stands.

The hybrid antecedents of the Children of Israel are not a mere matter of bookish record. Evidence of their hybrid descent is written all over them, wherever they are to be met with, so that in this respect the Jews of Europe are in the same case as the other Europeans, who are also universally cross-bred. It would perplex any anthropologist to identify a single individual among them all who could safely be set down as embodying the Jewish racial type without abatement. The variations in all the measurable traits that go to identify any individual in the schedules of the anthropologists are wide and ubiquitous as regards both their physical and their spiritual traits, in respect of anthropometric measurements as well as in temperament and capacities. And yet, when all is said in abatement of it, the Jewish type, it must be admitted, asserts itself with amazing persistence through all the disguises with which it has been overlaid in the course of age-long hybridization. Whatever may be found true elsewhere, in their contact with other racial types than those of Europe, it still appears that within this European racial environment the outcome given by any infusion of Jewish blood in these cross-bred individuals is something which can be identified as Jewish. Cross-breeding commonly results in a gain to the Jewish community rather than conversely; and the hybrid offspring is a child of Israel rather than of the gentiles.

In effect, therefore, it is the contribution of this Jewish-hybrid people to the culture of modern Europe that is in question. The men of this Jewish extraction count for more than their proportionate share in the intellectual life of western civilization; and they count particularly among the vanguard, the pioneers, the uneasy gild of pathfinders and iconoclasts, in science, scholarship and institutional change and growth. On its face it appears as if an infusion of Jewish blood, even in some degree of hybrid attenuation, were the one decisive factor in the case; and something of that sort may well be allowed, to avoid argument if for no more substantial reason. But even a casual survey of the available evidence will leave so broad a claim in doubt.

Of course, there is the fact to be allowed for at the outset, so far as need be, that these intellectuals of Jewish extraction are, after all, of hybrid extraction as well; but this feature of the case need be given no undue weight. It is of consequence in its bearing on the case of the Jews only in the same manner and degree as it is of consequence for any other hybrid people. Cross-breeding gives a wider range of variation and a greater diversity of individual endowment than can be had in any passably pure-bred population; from which results a greater effectual flexibility of aptitudes and capacities in such a people when exposed to conditions that make for change. In this respect the Jews are neither more nor less fortunate than their gentile compatriots.

It may be more to the purpose to note that this intellectual

pre-eminence of the Jews has come into bearing within the gentile
community of peoples, not from the outside; that the men who
have been its bearers have been men immersed in this gentile
culture in which they have played their part of guidance and
incitement, not bearers of a compelling message from afar or
proselyters of enlightenment conjuring with a ready formula worked
out in the ghetto and carried over into the gentile community for
its mental regeneration. In point of fact, neither these nor other
Jews have done effectual missionary work, in any ordinary sense
of that term, in this or any other connection; nor have they entertained a design to do so. Indeed, the Chosen People have quite
characteristically never been addicted to missionary enterprise; nor
does the Jewish scheme of right and honest living comprise anything of the kind. This, too, is notorious fact; so much so that
this allusion to it may well strike any Jew as foolish insistence on
a commonplace matter of course. In their character of a Chosen
People, it is not for them to take thought of their unblest neighbors
and seek to dispel the darkness that overlies the soul of the gentiles.

The cultural heritage of the Jewish people is large and rich,
and it is of ancient and honorable lineage. And from time immemorial this people has shown aptitude for such work as will tax
the powers of thought and imagination. Their home-bred achievements of the ancient time, before the Diaspora, are among the
secure cultural monuments of mankind; but these achievements
of the Jewish ancients neither touch the frontiers of modern science
nor do they fall in the lines of modern scholarship. So also the
later achievements of the Jewish scholars and savants, insofar as
their intellectual enterprise has gone forward on what may be
called distinctively Jewish lines, within the confines of their own
community and by the leading of their own home-bred interest,
untouched by that peculiar drift of inquiry that characterizes the
speculations of the modern gentile world—this learning of the
later generations of home-bred Jewish scholars is also reputed to
have run into lucubrations that have no significance for contemporary science or scholarship at large.

It appears to be only when the gifted Jew escapes from the
cultural environment created and fed by the particular genius of
his own people, only when he falls into the alien lines of gentile

inquiry and becomes a naturalized, though hyphenate, citizen in the gentile republic of learning, that he comes into his own as a creative leader in the world's intellectual enterprise. It is by loss of allegiance, or at the best by force of a divided allegiance to the people of his origin, that he finds himself in the vanguard of modern inquiry.

It will not do to say that none but renegade Jews count effectually in the modern sciences. Such a statement would be too broad; but, for all its excessive breadth, it exceeds the fact only by a margin. The margin may seem wide, so wide as to vitiate the general statement, perhaps, or at least wide enough materially to reduce its cogency. But it would be wider of the mark to claim that the renegades are to be counted only as sporadic exceptions among a body of unmitigated Jews who make up the virtual total of that muster of creative men of science which the Jewish people have thrown into the intellectual advance of Christendom.

The first requisite for constructive work in modern science, and indeed for any work of inquiry that shall bring enduring results, is a skeptical frame of mind. The enterprising skeptic alone can be counted on to further the increase of knowledge in any substantial fashion. This will be found true both in the modern sciences and in the field of scholarship at large. Much good and serviceable workmanship of a workday character goes into the grand total of modern scientific achievement; but that pioneering and engineering work of guidance, design, and theoretical correlation, without which the most painstaking collection and canvass of information is irrelevant, incompetent and impertinent—this intellectual enterprise that goes forward presupposes a degree of exemption from hard-and-fast preconceptions, a skeptical animus, *Unbefangenheit,* release from the dead hand of conventional finality.

The intellectually gifted Jew is in a peculiarly fortunate position in respect of this requisite immunity from the inhibitions of intellectual quietism. But he can come in for such immunity only at the cost of losing his secure place in the scheme of conventions into which he has been born, and at the cost, also, of finding no similarly secure place in that scheme of gentile conventions into which he is thrown. For him as for other men in the like case, the skepticism that goes to make him an effectual factor in the increase and diffusion of knowledge among men involves a loss of that peace of mind that is the birthright of the safe and sane quietist. He becomes a disturber of the intellectual peace, but only at the cost of becoming an intellectual wayfaring man, a wanderer in the intellectual no-man's land, seeking another place to rest, farther along the road, somewhere over the horizon. They are neither a complaisant nor a contented lot, these aliens of the uneasy feet; but that is, after all, not the point in question.

The young Jew who is at all gifted with a taste for knowledge will unavoidably go afield into that domain of learning where the gentile interests dominate and the gentile orientation gives the outcome. There is nowhere else to go on this quest. He comes forthwith to realize that the scheme of traditions and conventional verities handed down within the pale of his own people are matters of habit handed down by tradition, that they have only such force as belongs to matters of habit and convention, and that they lose their binding force so soon as the habitually accepted outlook is given up or seriously deranged. These nationally binding convictions of what is true, good and beautiful in the world of the human spirit are forthwith seen to be only contingently good and true; to be binding only so far as the habitual will to believe in them and to seek the truth along their lines remains intact. That is to say, only so long as no scheme of habituation alien to the man's traditional outlook has broken in on him, and has forced him to see that those convictions and verities which hold their place as fundamentally and eternally good and right within the balanced scheme of received traditions, prove to be, after all, only an ephemeral web of habits of thought; so soon as his current habits of life no longer continue to fall in those traditional lines that keep these habits of thought in countenance.

Now it happens that the home-bred Jewish scheme of things, human and divine, and the ways and means of knowledge that go with such a scheme, are of an archaic fashion, good and true, perhaps, beyond all praise, for the time and conditions that gave rise to it all, that wove that web of habituation and bound its close-knit tissue of traditional verities and conventions. But it all bears the date-mark, "B.C." It is of a divine complexion, monotheistic even, and perhaps intrinsically thearchic; it is ritualistic, with an exceedingly and beautifully magical efficacy of ritual necessity. It is imperiously self-balanced and self-sufficient, to the point of sanctity; and as is always true of such schemes of sanctity and magical sufficiency, it runs on a logic of personal and spiritual traits, qualities and relations, a class of imponderables which are no longer of the substance of those things that are inquired into by men to whom the ever increasingly mechanistic orientation of the modern time becomes habitual.

When the gifted young Jew, still flexible in respect of his mental habits, is set loose among the iron pots of this mechanistic orientation, the clay vessel of Jewish archaism suffers that fortune which is due and coming to clay vessels among the iron pots. His beautifully rounded heirloom, trade-marked "B.C.," goes to pieces between his hands, and they are left empty. He is divested of those archaic conventional preconceptions which will not comport with the intellectual environment in which he finds himself. But he is not thereby invested with the gentile's peculiar heritage of conventional preconceptions which have stood over, by inertia of habit, out of the gentile past, which go, on the one hand, to make the safe and sane gentile, conservative and complacent, and which conduce also, on the other hand, to blur the safe and sane gentile's intellectual vision, and to leave him intellectually sessile.

The young Jew finds his own heritage of usage and outlook untenable; but this does not mean that he therefore will take over and inwardly assimilate the traditions of usage and outlook which the gentile world has to offer; or at the most he does not uncritically take over all the intellectual prepossessions that are always standing over among the substantial citizens of the republic of learning. The idols of his own tribe have crumbled in decay and no longer cumber the ground, but that release does not induce him to set up a new line of idols borrowed from an alien tribe to do the same disservice. By consequence he is in a peculiar degree exposed to the unmediated facts of the current situation; and in a peculiar degree, therefore, he takes his orientation from the run of the facts as he finds them, rather than from the traditional interpretation of analogous facts in the past. In short, he is a skeptic by force of circumstances over which he has no control. Which comes to saying that he is in line to become a guide and leader of men in that intellectual enterprise out of which comes the increase and diffusion of knowledge among men, provided always that he is by native gift endowed with that net modicum of intelligence which takes effect in the play of the idle curiosity.

Intellectually he is likely to become an alien; spiritually he is more than likely to remain a Jew; for the heartstrings of affection and consuetude are tied early, and they are not readily retied in after life. Nor does the animus with which the community of safe and sane gentiles is wont to meet him conduce at all to his personal incorporation in that community, whatever may befall the intellectual assets which he brings. Their people need not become his people nor their gods his gods, and indeed the provocation is forever and irritably present all over the place to turn back from following after them. The most amiable share in the gentile community's life that is likely to fall to his lot is that of being interned. One who goes away from home will come to see many unfamiliar things, and to take note of them; but it does not follow that he will swear by all the strange gods whom he meets along the road.

As bearing on the Zionist's enterprise in isolation and nationality, this fable appears to teach a two-fold moral: If the adventure is carried to that consummate outcome which seems to be aimed at, it should apparently be due to be crowned with a large national complacency and, possibly, a profound and self-sufficient content on the part of the Chosen People domiciled once more in the Chosen Land; and when and insofar as the Jewish people in this way turn inward on themselves, their prospective contribution to the world's intellectual output should, in the light of the historical evidence, fairly be expected to take on the complexion of Talmudic lore, rather than that character of free-swung skeptical initiative which their renegades have habitually infused into the pursuit of the modern sciences abroad among the nations. Doubtless, even so the supply of Jewish renegades would not altogether cease, though it should presumably fall off to a relatively inconsiderable residue. And not all renegades are fit guides and leaders of men on the quest of knowledge, nor is their dominant incentive always or ordinarily the quest of the idle curiosity.

There should be some loss to Christendom at large, and there might be some gain to the repatriated Children of Israel. It is a sufficiently difficult choice between a life of complacent futility at home and a thankless quest of unprofitable knowledge abroad. It is, after all, a matter of the drift of circumstance; and behind that lies a question of taste, about which there is no disputing.

The Century's Great Men in Science

CHARLES S. PEIRCE

Charles Sanders Peirce (1839–1914) is now not even a name to the general public, but William James called him the most original mind of their generation and his reputation among philosophers is still rising. His academic career, however, was even more dismal than Veblen's. He was born into an old Boston family, and his father was professor of mathematics and astronomy at Harvard. Peirce got a degree in chemistry *summa cum laude* from Harvard in 1863, two years after he had begun working for the United States Coast Survey. He stayed with the Survey for thirty years, during which he had only brief and minor university jobs. Much of his best work remained unpublished until after he died, and for the last twenty-five years of his life he pieced together a livelihood by work ranging from private tutoring to translating to writing for dictionaries and encyclopedias. The following analysis is reprinted from the *Annual Report of the Smithsonian Institution for the Year Ending June 30, 1900* (Washington, 1901).

How SHALL we determine that men are great? Who, for instance, shall we say are the great men of science? The men who have made the great and fruitful discoveries? Such discoveries in the nineteenth century have mostly been made independently by two or more persons. Darwin and Wallace simultaneously put forth the hypothesis of natural selection. Clausius, Rankine, and Sadi-Carnot, perhaps Kelvin, worked out the mechanical theory of heat. Krönig, Clausius, Joule, Herapath, Waterston, and Daniel Bernouilli independently suggested the kinetical theory of gases.

I do not know how many minds besides Robert Mayer, Colding, Joule, and Helmholtz hit upon the doctrine of the conservation of energy. Faraday and Joseph Henry brought magneto-electricity to light. The pack of writers who were on the warm scent of the periodic law of the chemical elements approached two hundred when the discovery itself, a most difficult inference, was partly achieved by Lothar Meyer, wholly by Mendeléef. When great discoveries were thus in the air, shall that brain necessarily be deemed great upon which they happened earliest to condense, or the man supereminent who, by the unmeaning rule of priority of publication, gets the credit in brief statements? No, this method of estimation, natural as it is to make success the standard of measure, will not do.

Shall we, then, by a logical analysis, draw up an abstract definition of greatness and call those men great who conform to it? If there were no dispute about the nature of greatness, this might probably prove the most convenient plan. It would be like a rule of grammar adduced to decide whether a phrase is good English or not. Nor would the circumstance that the definition could not be as explicit and determinate as a rule of grammar constitute a serious difficulty. Unfortunately, however, among the few writers who have seriously studied the question, the most extreme differences prevail as to the nature of great men. Some hold that they are fashioned of the most ordinary clay, and that only their rearing and environment, conjoined with fortunate opportunities, make them what they are. The heaviest weight, intellectually, among these writers maintains, on the other hand, that circumstances are as powerless to suppress the great man as they would be to subject a human being to a nation of dogs. But it was only the blundering Malvolio who got the notion that some are born great. The sentence of the astute Maria was: "Some are become great: some atcheeves greatnesse, and some have greatnesse thrust uppon em." Amid this difference of opinion any definition of greatness would be like a disputed rule of grammar. Just as a rule of grammar does not render an expression bad English, but only generalizes the fact that good writers do not use it so, in order to establish a definition of greatness, it would be necessary to begin by ascertaining what men were and what men were not great, and that having been done the rule might as well be dispensed with. My opinion will, I fear, be set down by some intellectual men as foolishness, though it has not been lightly formed nor without long years of experimentation—that the way to judge of whether a man was great or not is to put aside all analysis, to contemplate attentively his life and works, and then to look into one's heart and estimate the impression one finds to have been made. This is the way in which one would decide whether a mountain were sublime or not. The great man is the impressive personality, and the question whether he is great is a question of impression.

The glory of the nineteenth century has been its science, and its scientific great men are those whom I mean here to consider. Their distinctive characteristic throughout the century, and more and more so in each succeeding generation, has been devotion to the pursuit of truth for truth's sake. In this century we have not heard a Franklin asking, "What signifies a philosophy which does not apply itself to some use?"—a remark that could be paralleled by utterances of Laplace, of Rumford, of Buffon, and of many another well-qualified spokesman of eighteenth-century science. It was in the early dawn of the nineteenth that Gauss (or was it Dirichlet?) gave as the reason of his passion for the Theory of Numbers that "it is a pure virgin that never has been and never can be prostituted to any practical application whatsoever." It was my inestimable privilege to have felt as a boy the warmth of the steadily burning enthusiasm of the scientific generation of Darwin, most of the leaders of which at home I knew intimately and some very well in almost every country of Europe. I particularize that generation without having any reason to suspect that that flame has since burned dimmer or less purely, but simply because if a word belonged to one's mother tongue, one may be supposed to know unerringly the meaning the teachers of one's boyhood attached to it.

The word science was one often in those men's mouths, and I am quite sure they did not mean by it "systematized knowledge," as former ages had defined it, nor anything set down in a book; but, on the contrary, a mode of life; not knowledge, but the devoted, well-considered life pursuit of knowledge; devotion to

truth—not "devotion to truth as one sees it," for that is no devotion to truth at all, but only to party—no, far from that, devotion
to the truth that the man is not yet able to see but is striving to
obtain. The word was thus, from the etymological point of view,
already a misnomer. And so it remains with the scientists of today.
What they meant and still mean by "science" ought, etymologi-
cally, to be called philosophy. But during the nineteenth century
it was only a metaphysical professor of a now obsolescent type,
as I hope, who could sit in his academic chair, puffed up with
his "systematized knowledge"—no true philosopher, but a mere
philodoxer. For a snapshot at the nineteenth-century man of
science one may take Sir Humphrey Davy, willing, as early as 1818,
seriously to investigate the liquefaction of the blood of St. Janu-
arius; or John Tyndall, with scientific ingenuousness proposing
that prayer test to which no clerical Elijah has yet been found
with the faith and good faith to respond; or William Crookes,
devoting years of his magnificent powers to examining the supposed evidences of the direct action of mind upon matter in the
face of the world's scorn. Contrast these instances with the refusal
of Laplace and Biot in the closing years of the previous century
to accept the evidence that stones fall from heaven (evidence prov-
ing that they do so daily), simply because their prepossessions
were the other way. One of the geologist brothers De Luc declared
that he would not believe such a thing though he saw it with his
own eyes; and a scientifically given English ecclesiastic who
happened to be sojourning in Siena when a shower of aerolites
were dashed in broad daylight into an open square of that town,
wrote home that having seen the stones he had found the testimony
of eyewitnesses so unimpeachable and so trustworthy that—that he
accepted the fact, you will say? by no means—that he knew not
what to think! Such was the bon sens that guided the eighteenth
century—a pretty phrase for ineradicable prejudice.

To this self-effacement before the grandeur of reason and truth
is traceable the greatness of nineteenth-century science, most obviously in mathematics. In the minds of eighteenth-century mathematicians their science existed for the sake of its applications.
Forgetfulness of this was in their eyes reprehensible, immoral.
The question was, what would a given piece of mathematics do?

They liked smooth-running and elegant machinery—there was economy in that; but they were not sedulous that it should have symmetry; idle admiration of its beauty they hardly approved. If it was excessively complicated and intricate, that was regarded rather as a feature to be proud of than as a blemish. Were the complete revolution that the nineteenth century wrought upon the ideal of mathematics not notorious, one could soon convince himself of it by looking over almost any modern treatise—say, Salmon on Higher Plane Curves. That volume, for example, would be found replete with theorems hardly any of which hold good for any curves that could really exist. Realizable curves have hardly been studied at all, for the reason that they do not yield a beautiful theory, such as is now exacted. Modern mathematics is highly artistic. A simple theme is chosen, some conception pretty and charming in itself. Then it is shown that by simply holding this idea up to one's eye and looking through it a whole forest that before seemed a thick and tangled jungle of brushes and briers is seen to be in reality an orderly garden. The word generalization really cannot be fully understood without studying modern mathematics; nor can the beauty of generalization be in any other way so well appreciated. There is here no need of throwing out "extreme cases." Far from that, it is precisely in the extreme cases that the power and beauty of the magic eyeglass is most apparent and most marvellous. Let me take back the word "magic," though, for the reasonableness of it is just its crowning charm. I must not be led away from my point, to expatiate upon the reposefulness of the new mathematics, upon how it relieves us of that tiresome imp, man, and from the most importunate and unsatisfactory of the race, one's self. Suffice it to say that it is so reasonable, so simple, so easy to read, when the right view has once been attained, that the student may easily forget what arduous labors were expended in constructing the first convenient pathway to that lofty summit, that mastery over intricacies, far beyond that of the eighteenth-century master. "It must not be supposed," said C. G. J. Jacobi, one of the simplifying pioneers, "that it is to a gift of nature that I owe such mathematical power as I possess. No; it has come by hard work, hard work. Not mere industry, but brain-splitting thinking—hard work; hard work that

has often endangered my health." Such reflections enable us to
perceive that if modern mathematics is great, so also were the
men who made it great.

The science next in abstractness after mathematics is logic.
The contributions of the eighteenth century to this subject were
enormous. In pure logic the doctrine of chances, which has been
the logical guide of the exact sciences and is now illuminating the
pathway of the theory of evolution, and is destined to still higher
uses, received at the hands of Jacob Bernouilli and of Laplace
developments of the first importance. In the theory of cognition
Berkeley and Kant laid solid foundations; their personal greatness
is incontestable. This is hardly true of Hume. In the nineteenth
century Boole created a method of miraculous fruitfulness, which
aided in the development of the logic of relatives, and threw
great light on the doctrine of probability, and thereby upon the
theory and rules of inductive reasoning. De Morgan added an
entirely new kind of syllogism, and brought the logic of relatives
into existence, which revolutionizes general conceptions of reasoning. The works of Comte, Whewell, J. S. Mill, Jevons, and others
upon the philosophy of inductive science were less successful or
fruitful. In the more metaphysical part of logic the philosophy of
Hegel, though it cannot be accepted on the whole, was the work
of a great man. In metaphysics and general cosmology the attitude
of the century has been expectant. Herbert Spencer has been
proclaimed as a sort of scientific Messiah by a group of followers
more ardent than philosophic, which does not seem to be gathering
strength.

At the head of the physical sciences stands nomological physics.
Dr. Thomas Young was here the earliest great man of the century,
whose intellect illuminated every corner to which it was directed,
taking the first difficult steps in the decipherment of the hiero-
glyphics, originating the doctrine of color-mixtures, propounding
the correct theory of light, and illuminative everywhere. It gives
a realizing sense of the century's progress that this great man in
its early years should have opined that experimentation in general
had then been pushed about far enough. On that occasion it was
not his usual logic, but the eighteenth-century watchword "le bon
sens," that was his guide, with the sort of result it is continually

turning out when used beyond its proper sphere of every-day practical affairs. The advance of years, with their experience, has led physicists to expend more and vastly more effort upon extreme precision, against every protest of good sense. What has come of it? Marconi's wireless telegraphy, for one thing. For it was the precision with which the velocity of light on the one hand and the ratio of statical and dynamical constants of electricity on the other had been determined that proved to Maxwell that the vibrating medium of light was the substance of electricity, a theory that his great follower, Hertz, applied to making giant light waves less affected by obstructions than even those of sound. I dare say, sapient "good sense" pooh-poohs those wonderful new substances, helium and the rest, that seem the connecting link between ordinary matter and the ether. So it would be useless to point out that their discovery was entirely due to Lord Rayleigh's fastidiousness in the determination of the density of nitrogen. But it has to be noted as a characteristic of the great physicists of the nineteenth century that their reverence for every feature of the phenomenon, however minute, has been in thorough disaccord with the older "good sense." The greatest advances in physics during the century were made by several men at once. Certain ideas would come somehow to be in the air; and by the time they had crystallized for a student here and there, he would hesitate to announce as original conceptions what he had reason to suppose many men shared, while he knew that the larger body would not be yet ready to accept them. Under those circumstances priority of publication can signify nothing except haste.

Of all men of the century Faraday had the greatest power of drawing ideas straight out of his experiments and making his physical apparatus do his thinking, so that experimentation and inference were not two proceedings, but one. To understand what this means, read his "Researches on Electricity." His genius was thus higher than that of Helmholtz, who fitted a phenomenon with an appropriate conception out of his store, as one might fit a bottle with a stopper. The most wonderful capacity for "catching on" to the ideas of nature when these were of a complicated kind was shown by Mendeléef in making out the periodic law of the chemical elements, as one might make out the meaning of a pantomime, from data so fragmentary, and in some cases erroneous, that the interpretation involved the correction of sundry facts, corrections since confirmed, as well as the prediction of the very peculiar properties of the unknown gallium, scandium, and germanium, which were soon afterwards actually met with. Minute examination of all his utterances convinces one that Mendeléef's mental processes in this unparalleled induction were largely subconscious and, as such, indicate an absorption of the man's whole being in his devotion to the reason in facts.

A great naturalist, as well as I can make out, is a man whose capacious skull allows of his being on the alert to a hundred different things at once, this same alertness being connected with a power of seeing the relations between different complicated sets of phenomena when they are presented in their entirety. The eighteenth century had its Linnæus, whose greatness even I can detect as I turn over his pages; its Huber, discovering through others' eyes what others could not discern with their own; its Goethe, its Haller, its Hunter, and mixed with practical greatness, its Pinel and its Jenner. Then, there was Lavater, who showed how pure æsthetic estimation might be turned to the discovery of truth —a man depreciated because logicians and philodoxers can so much more easily detect his weakness than discern his strength. The nineteenth century, with its great thinker, Darwin; its Pasteur (great in chemistry as well as in biology, a man who impressed me personally, and impresses me in his works, as much as any but two or three of the century); its Lamaroll, Weissmann, Cuvier, Agassiz, von Baer, Bichat, Johannes Müller, Robert Brown, and I know not whom besides, has certainly garnered a magnificent harvest of great men from this field.

Those sciences which study individual objects and seek to explain them upon physical principles—astronomy, geology, etc., corresponding to history and biography on the psychical side— demand the greatest assemblage of different powers. Those who pursue them have first to be mathematicians, physicists, chemists, naturalists, all at once, and, after that, astronomers or geologists in addition. It is almost beyond human power. In the eighteenth century A. G. Werner broke ground in geology, William Herschel, Kant, and Laplace did great things in astronomy. In the nineteenth century geology was first really made a science, and among its great men one recalls at once Lyell, Agassiz, Kelvin. This country has become its home. In astronomy, too, this country has been eminent, especially in the new astronomy which has afforded the needed scope for greatness, instead of the narrow rut that Bessel and Argelander had left behind them. Thus it happens that we have a magnificent group of great astronomers living among us to-day. We stand too close to them to take in their true proportions. But it is certain that the names of Chandler, Langley, Newcomb, Pickering, and several others are indelibly inscribed upon the heavens. In England it is only this year that Sir Norman Lockyer has brought the extraordinary research to which his life has been devoted to completion, so far as such work can be said to be capable of completion. It is an attribute of its greatness that it is endless.

When we compare all the men I have glanced at, with a view to eliciting a common trait somewhat distinctive of the nineteenth century, we cannot but see that science has been animated by a new spirit, till the very word has become a misnomer. It is the man of science, eager to have his every opinion regenerated, his every idea rationalized, by drinking at the fountain of fact, and devoting all the energies of his life to the cult of truth, not as he understands it, but as he does not yet understand it, that ought properly to be called a philosopher. To an earlier age knowledge was power, merely that and nothing more; to us it is life and the summum bonum. Emancipation from the bonds of self, of one's own prepossessions, importunately sought at the hands of that rational power before which all must ultimately bow—this is the characteristic that distinguishes all the great figures of the nineteenth-century science from those of former periods.

The Path of the Law

OLIVER WENDELL HOLMES, JR.

Oliver Wendell Holmes, Jr., son of the physician and poet, was born in 1841 in Boston and educated at Harvard, as his ancestors had been. He served with the Union Army in the Civil War and was wounded three times. In 1866 he got his law degree from Harvard and went off to Europe for a year—the first of many such trips. He practiced law in Boston while writing *The Common Law* (1882); its publication caused a professorship to be established for him at the Harvard Law School. Later the same year he became associate justice of the highest court in Massachusetts, and, in 1899, chief justice. On December 8, 1902, by appointment of Theodore Roosevelt, he took his seat on the bench of the Supreme Court of the United States, where he remained for thirty years. He died in 1935. This address was given at the Boston University School of Law on January 8, 1897, and first published in the *Harvard Law Review*, X (1897).

WHEN WE study law we are not studying a mystery but a well-known profession. We are studying what we shall want in order to appear before judges, or to advise people in such a way as to keep them out of court. The reason why it is a profession, why people will pay lawyers to argue for them or to advise them, is that in societies like ours the command of the public force is intrusted to the judges in certain cases, and the whole power of the state will be put forth, if necessary, to carry out their judgments and decrees. People want to know under what circumstances and how far they will run the risk of coming against what is so much stronger than themselves, and hence it becomes a business to find out when this danger is to be feared. The object of our study, then, is prediction, the prediction of the incidence of the public force through the instrumentality of the courts.

The means of the study are a body of reports, of treatises, and of statutes, in this country and in England, extending back for six hundred years, and now increasing annually by hundreds. In these sibylline leaves are gathered the scattered prophecies of the past upon the cases in which the axe will fall. These are what properly have been called the oracles of the law. Far the most important and pretty nearly the whole meaning of every new effort of legal thought is to make these prophecies more precise, and to generalize them into a thoroughly connected system. The process is one, from a lawyer's statement of a case, eliminating as it does all the dramatic elements with which his client's story has clothed it, and retaining only the facts of legal import, up to the final analyses and abstract universals of theoretic jurisprudence. The reason why a lawyer does not mention that his client wore a white hat when he made a contract, while Mrs. Quickly would be sure to dwell upon it along with the parcel gilt goblet and the sea-coal fire, is that he foresees that the public force will act in the same way whatever his client had upon his head. It is to make the prophecies easier to be remembered and to be understood that the teachings of the decisions of the past are put into general propositions and gathered into text-books, or that statutes are passed in a general form. The primary rights and duties with which jurisprudence busies itself again are nothing but prophecies. One of the many evil effects of the confusion between legal and moral ideas, about which I shall have something to say in a moment, is that theory is apt to get the cart before the horse, and to consider the right or the duty as something existing apart from and independent of the consequences of its breach, to which certain sanctions are added afterward. But, as I shall try to show, a legal duty so called is nothing but a prediction that if a man does or omits certain things he will be made to suffer in this or that way by judgment of the court;—and so of a legal right.

The number of our predictions when generalized and reduced to a system is not unmanageably large. They present themselves as a finite body of dogma which may be mastered within a reasonable time. It is a great mistake to be frightened by the ever increasing number of reports. The reports of a given jurisdiction in the course of a generation take up pretty much the whole body of the law, and restate it from the present point of view. We could reconstruct the corpus from them if all that went before were burned. The use of the earlier reports is mainly historical, a use about which I shall have something to say before I have finished.

I wish, if I can, to lay down some first principles for the study of this body of dogma or systematized prediction which we call the law, for men who want to use it as the instrument of their business to enable them to prophesy in their turn, and, as bearing upon the study, I wish to point out an ideal which as yet our law has not attained.

The first thing for a business-like understanding of the matter is to understand its limits, and therefore I think it desirable at once to point out and dispel a confusion between morality and law, which sometimes rises to the height of conscious theory, and more often and indeed constantly is making trouble in detail without reaching the point of consciousness. You can see very plainly that a bad man has as much reason as a good one for wishing to avoid an encounter with the public force, and therefore you can see the practical importance of the distinction between morality and law. A man who cares nothing for an ethical rule which is believed and practiced by his neighbors is likely nevertheless to care a good deal to avoid being made to pay money, and will want to keep out of jail if he can.

I take it for granted that no hearer of mine will misinterpret what I have to say as the language of cynicism. The law is the witness and external deposit of our moral life. Its history is the history of the moral development of the race. The practice of it, in spite of popular jests, tends to make good citizens and good men. When I emphasize the difference between law and morals I do so with reference to a single end, that of learning and understanding the law. For that purpose you must definitely master its specific marks, and it is for that that I ask you for the moment to imagine yourselves indifferent to other and greater things.

I do not say that there is not a wider point of view from which the distinction between law and morals becomes of secondary or no importance, as all mathematical distinctions vanish in presence of the infinite. But I do say that that distinction is of the first importance for the object which we are here to consider,— a right study and mastery of the law as a business with well understood limits, a body of dogma enclosed within definite lines. I have just shown the practical reason for saying so. If you want to know the law and nothing else, you must look at it as a bad man, who cares only for the material consequences which such knowledge enables him to predict, not as a good one, who finds his reasons for conduct, whether inside the law or outside of it, in the vaguer sanctions of conscience. The theoretical importance of the distinction is no less, if you would reason on your subject aright. The law is full of phraseology drawn from morals, and by the mere force of language continually invites us to pass from one domain to the other without perceiving it, as we are sure to do unless we have the boundary constantly before our minds. The law talks about rights, and duties, and malice, and intent, and negligence, and so forth; and nothing is easier, or, I may say, more common in legal reasoning, than to take these words in their moral sense, at some stage of the argument, and so to drop into fallacy. For instance, when we speak of the rights of man in a moral sense, we mean to mark the limits of interference with individual freedom which we think are prescribed by conscience, or by our ideal, however reached. Yet it is certain that many laws have been enforced in the past, and it is likely that some are enforced now, which are condemned by the most enlightened opinion of the time, or which at all events pass the limit of interference as many consciences would draw it. Manifestly, therefore, nothing but confusion of thought can result from assuming that the rights of man in a moral sense are equally rights in the sense of the Constitution and the law. No doubt simple and extreme cases can be put of imaginable laws which the statute-making power would not dare to enact, even in the absence of written constitutional prohibitions, because the community would rise in rebellion and fight; and this gives some plausibility to the proposition that the law, if not a part of morality, is limited by it. But this limit of power is not coextensive with any system of morals.

For the most part it falls far within the lines of any such system, and in some cases may extend beyond them, for reasons drawn from the habits of a particular people at a particular time. I once heard the late Professor Agassiz say that a German population would rise if you added two cents to the price of a glass of beer. A statute in such a case would be empty words, not because it was wrong, but because it could not be enforced. No one will deny that wrong statutes can be and are enforced, and we should not all agree as to which were the wrong ones.

The confusion with which I am dealing besets confessedly legal conceptions. Take the fundamental question, What constitutes the law? You will find some text writers telling you that it is something different from what is decided by the courts of Massachusetts or England, that it is a system of reason, that it is a deduction from principles of ethics or admitted axioms or what not, which may or may not coincide with the decisions. But if we take the view of our friend the bad man, we shall find that he does not care two straws for the axioms or deductions, but that he does want to know what the Massachusetts or English courts are likely to do in fact. I am much of his mind. The prophecies of what the courts will do in fact, and nothing more pretentious, are what I mean by the law.

Take again a notion which as popularly understood is the widest conception which the law contains;—the notion of legal duty, to which already I have referred. We fill the word with all the content which we draw from morals. But what does it mean to a bad man? Mainly, and in the first place, a prophecy that if he does certain things he will be subjected to disagreeable consequences by way of imprisonment or compulsory payment of money. But from his point of view, what is the difference between being fined and being taxed a certain sum for doing a certain thing? That his point of view is the test of legal principles is shown by the many discussions which have arisen in the courts on the very question whether a given statutory liability is a penalty or a tax. On the answer to this question depends the decision whether conduct is legally wrong or right, and also whether a man is under compulsion or free. Leaving the criminal law on one side, what is the difference between the liability under the mill acts or statutes

authorizing a taking by eminent domain and the liability for what
we call a wrongful conversion of property where restoration is
out of the question? In both cases the party taking another man's
property has to pay its fair value as assessed by a jury, and no
more. What significance is there in calling one taking right and
another wrong from the point of view of the law? It does not
matter, so far as the given consequence, the compulsory payment,
is concerned, whether the act to which it is attached is described
in terms of praise or in terms of blame, or whether the law purports
to prohibit it or to allow it. If it matters at all, still speaking from
the bad man's point of view, it must be because in one case and
not in the other some further disadvantages, or at least some further
consequences, are attached to the act by the law. The only other
disadvantages thus attached to it which I ever have been able to
think of are to be found in two somewhat insignificant legal doctrines, both of which might be abolished without much disturbance.
One is, that a contract to do a prohibited act is unlawful, and
the other, that, if one of two or more joint wrongdoers has to pay
all the damages, he cannot recover contribution from his fellows.
And that I believe is all. You see how the vague circumference of
the notion of duty shrinks and at the same time grows more
precise when we wash it with cynical acid and expel everything
except the object of our study, the operations of the law.

Nowhere is the confusion between legal and moral ideas more
manifest than in the law of contract. Among other things, here
again the so-called primary rights and duties are invested with a
mystic significance beyond what can be assigned and explained.
The duty to keep a contract at common law means a prediction
that you must pay damages if you do not keep it,—and nothing
else. If you commit a tort, you are liable to pay a compensatory
sum. If you commit a contract, you are liable to pay a compensatory sum unless the promised event comes to pass, and that is
all the difference. But such a mode of looking at the matter stinks
in the nostrils of those who think it advantageous to get as much
ethics into the law as they can. It was good enough for Lord
Coke, however, and here, as in many other cases, I am content to
abide with him. In Bromage v. Genning,[1] a prohibition was sought

[1] Roll. Rep. 368.

in the King's Bench against a suit in the marches of Wales for
the specific performance of a covenant to grant a lease, and Coke
said that it would subvert the intention of the covenantor, since
he intends it to be at his election either to lose the damages or
to make the lease. Sergeant Harris for the plaintiff confessed that
he moved the matter against his conscience, and a prohibition
was granted. This goes further than we should go now, but it shows
what I venture to say has been the common-law point of view
from the beginning, although Mr. Harriman, in his very able little
book upon Contracts, has been misled, as I humbly think, to a
different conclusion.

I have spoken only of the common law, because there are some
cases in which a logical justification can be found for speaking of
civil liabilities as imposing duties in an intelligible sense. These
are the relatively few in which equity will grant an injunction, and
will enforce it by putting the defendant in prison or otherwise
punishing him unless he complies with the order of the court.
But I hardly think it advisable to shape general theory from the
exception, and I think it would be better to cease troubling ourselves about primary rights and sanctions altogether, than to
describe our prophecies concerning the liabilities commonly imposed by the law in those inappropriate terms.

I mentioned, as other examples of the use by the law of words
drawn from morals, malice, intent, and negligence. It is enough to
take malice as it is used in the law of civil liability for wrongs,—
what we lawyers call the law of torts,—to show you that it means
something different in law from what it means in morals, and
also to show how the difference has been obscured by giving to
principles which have little or nothing to do with each other the
same name. Three hundred years ago a parson preached a sermon
and told a story out of Fox's *Book of Martyrs* of a man who
had assisted at the torture of one of the saints, and afterward died,
suffering compensatory inward torment. It happened that Fox
was wrong. The man was alive and chanced to hear the sermon,
and thereupon he sued the parson. Chief Justice Wray instructed
the jury that the defendant was not liable, because the story was
told innocently, without malice. He took malice in the moral sense,

as importing a malevolent motive. But nowadays no one doubts that a man may be liable, without any malevolent motive at all, for false statements manifestly calculated to inflict temporal damage. In stating the case in pleading, we still should call the defendant's conduct malicious; but, in my opinion at least, the word means nothing about motives, or even about the defendant's attitude toward the future, but only signifies that the tendency of his conduct under the known circumstances was very plainly to cause the plaintiff temporal harm.[2]

In the law of contract the use of moral phraseology has led to equal confusion, as I have shown in part already, but only in part. Morals deal with the actual internal state of the individual's mind, what he actually intends. From the time of the Romans down to now, this mode of dealing has affected the language of the law as to contract, and the language used has reacted upon the thought. We talk about a contract as a meeting of the minds of the parties, and thence it is inferred in various cases that there is no contract because their minds have not met; that is, because they have intended different things or because one party has not known of the assent of the other. Yet nothing is more certain than that parties may be bound by a contract to things which neither of them intended, and when one does not know of the other's assent. Suppose a contract is executed in due form and in writing to deliver a lecture, mentioning no time. One of the parties thinks that the promise will be construed to mean at once, within a week. The other thinks that it means when he is ready. The court says that it means within a reasonable time. The parties are bound by the contract as it is interpreted by the court, yet neither of them meant what the court declares that they have said. In my opinion no one will understand the true theory of contract or be able even to discuss some fundamental questions intelligently until he has understood that all contracts are formal, that the making of a contract depends not on the agreement of two minds in one intention but on the agreement of two sets of external signs,— not on the parties' having *meant* the same things but on their having *said* the same thing. Furthermore, as the signs may be addressed to one sense or another,—to sight or to hearing,—on

[2] See Hanson v. Globe Newspaper Co., 159 Mass. 293, 302.

the nature of the sign will depend the moment when the contract is made. If the sign is tangible, for instance a letter, the contract is made when the letter of acceptance is delivered. If it is necessary that the minds of the parties meet, there will be no contract until the acceptance can be read,—none, for example, if the acceptance be snatched from the hand of the offerer by a third person.

This is not the time to work out a theory in detail, or to answer many obvious doubts and questions which are suggested by these general views. I know of none which are not easy to answer, but what I am trying to do now is only by a series of hints to throw some light on the narrow path of legal doctrine, and upon two pitfalls which, as it seems to me, lie perilously near to it. Of the first of these I have said enough. I hope that my illustrations have shown the danger, both to speculation and to practice, of confounding morality with law, and the trap which legal language lays for us on that side of our way. For my own part, I often doubt whether it would not be a gain if every word of moral significance could be banished from the law altogether, and other words adopted which should convey legal ideas uncolored by anything outside the law. We should lose the fossil records of a good deal of history and the majesty got from ethical associations, but by ridding ourselves of an unnecessary confusion we should gain very much in the clearness of our thought.

So much for the limits of the law. The next thing which I wish to consider is what are the forces which determine its content and its growth. You may assume, with Hobbes and Bentham and Austin, that all law emanates from the sovereign, even when the first human beings to enunciate it are the judges, or you may think that law is the voice of the *Zeitgeist*, or what you like. It is all one to my present purpose. Even if every decision required the sanction of an emperor with despotic power and a whimsical turn of mind, we should be interested none the less, still with a view to prediction, in discovering some order, some rational explanation, and some principle of growth for the rules which he laid down. In every system there are such explanations and principles to be found. It is with regard to them that a second fallacy comes in, which I think it important to expose.

The fallacy to which I refer is the notion that the only force at work in the development of the law is logic. In the broadest sense, indeed, that notion would be true. The postulate on which we think about the universe is that there is a fixed quantitative relation between every phenomenon and its antecedents and consequents. If there is such a thing as a phenomenon without these fixed quantitative relations, it is a miracle. It is outside the law of cause and effect, and as such transcends our power of thought, or at least is something to or from which we cannot reason. The condition of our thinking about the universe is that it is capable of being thought about rationally, or, in other words, that every part of it is effect and cause in the same sense in which those parts are with which we are most familiar. So in the broadest sense it is true that the law is a logical development, like everything else. The danger of which I speak is not the admission that the principles governing other phenomena also govern the law, but the notion that a given system, ours, for instance, can be worked out like mathematics from some general axioms of conduct. This is the natural error of the schools, but it is not confined to them. I once heard a very eminent judge say that he never let a decision go until he was absolutely sure that it was right. So judicial dissent often is blamed, as if it meant simply that one side or the other were not doing their sums right, and, if they would take more trouble, agreement inevitably would come.

This mode of thinking is entirely natural. The training of lawyers is a training in logic. The processes of analogy, discrimination, and deduction are those in which they are most at home. The language of judicial decision is mainly the language of logic. And the logical method and form flatter that longing for certainty and for repose which is in every human mind. But certainty generally is illusion, and repose is not the destiny of man. Behind the logical form lies a judgment as to the relative worth and importance of competing legislative grounds, often an inarticulate and unconscious judgment, it is true, and yet the very root and nerve of the whole proceeding. You can give any conclusion a logical form. You always can imply a condition in a contract. But why do you imply it? It is because of some belief as to the practice of the community or of a class, or because of some opinion as to policy, or, in short, because of some attitude of yours upon a matter not capable of exact quantitative measurement, and therefore not capable of founding exact logical conclusions. Such matters really are battle grounds where the means do not exist for determinations that shall be good for all time, and where the decision can do no more than embody the preference of a given body in a given time and place. We do not realize how large a part of our law is open to reconsideration upon a slight change in the habit of the public mind. No concrete proposition is self-evident, no matter how ready we may be to accept it, not even Mr. Herbert Spencer's Every man has a right to do what he wills, provided he interferes not with a like right on the part of his neighbors.

Why is a false and injurious statement privileged, if it is made honestly in giving information about a servant? It is because it has been thought more important that information should be given freely, than that a man should be protected from what under other circumstances would be an actionable wrong. Why is a man at liberty to set up a business which he knows will ruin his neighbor? It is because the public good is supposed to be best subserved by free competition. Obviously such judgments of relative importance may vary in different times and places. Why does a judge instruct a jury that an employer is not liable to an employee for an injury received in the course of his employment unless he is negligent, and why do the jury generally find for the plaintiff if the case is allowed to go to them? It is because the traditional policy of our law is to confine liability to cases where a prudent man might have foreseen the injury, or at least the danger, while the inclination of a very large part of the community is to make certain classes of persons insure the safety of those with whom they deal. Since the last words were written, I have seen the requirement of such insurance put forth as part of the programme of one of the best known labor organizations. There is a concealed, half conscious battle on the question of legislative policy, and if anyone thinks that it can be settled deductively, or once for all, I only can say that I think he is theoretically wrong, and that I am certain that his conclusion will not be accepted in practice *semper ubique et ab omnibus*.

Indeed, I think that even now our theory upon this matter is open to reconsideration, although I am not prepared to say how I should decide if a reconsideration were proposed. Our law of torts comes from the old days of isolated, ungeneralized wrongs, assaults, slanders, and the like, where the damages might be taken to lie where they fell by legal judgment. But the torts with which our courts are kept busy to-day are mainly the incidents of certain well known businesses. They are injuries to person or property by railroads, factories, and the like. The liability for them is estimated, and sooner or later goes into the price paid by the public. The public really pays the damages, and the question of liability, if pressed far enough, is really the question how far it is desirable that the public should insure the safety of those whose work it uses. It might be said that in such cases the chance of a jury finding for the defendant is merely a chance, once in a while rather arbitrarily interrupting the regular course of recovery, most likely in the case of an unusually conscientious plaintiff, and therefore better done away with. On the other hand, the economic value even of a life to the community can be estimated, and no recovery, it may be said, ought to go beyond that amount. It is conceivable that some day in certain cases we may find ourselves imitating, on a higher plane, the tariff for life and limb which we see in the Leges Barbarorum.

I think that the judges themselves have failed adequately to recognize their duty of weighing considerations of social advantage. The duty is inevitable, and the result of the often proclaimed judicial aversion to deal with such considerations is simply to leave the very ground and foundation of judgments inarticulate, and often unconscious, as I have said. When socialism first began to be talked about, the comfortable classes of the community were a good deal frightened. I suspect that this fear has influenced judicial action both here and in England, yet it is certain that it is not a conscious factor in the decisions to which I refer. I think that something similar has led people who no longer hope to control the legislatures to look to the courts as expounders of the Constitutions, and that in some courts new principles have been discovered outside the bodies of those instruments, which may be generalized into acceptance of the economic doctrines which prevailed about fifty years ago, and a wholesale prohibition of what a tribunal of lawyers does not think about right. I cannot but believe that if the training of lawyers led them habitually to consider more definitely and explicitly the social advantage on which the rule they lay down must be justified, they sometimes would hesitate where now they are confident, and see that really they were taking sides upon debatable and often burning questions.

So much for the fallacy of logical form. Now let us consider the present condition of the law as a subject for study, and the ideal toward which it tends. We still are far from the point of view which I desire to see reached. No one has reached it or can reach it as yet. We are only at the beginning of a philosophical reaction, and of a reconsideration of the worth of doctrines which for the most part still are taken for granted without any deliberate, conscious, and systematic questioning of their grounds. The development of our law has gone on for nearly a thousand years, like the development of a plant, each generation taking the inevitable next step, mind, like matter, simply obeying a law of spontaneous growth. It is perfectly natural and right that it should have been so. Imitation is a necessity of human nature, as has been illustrated by a remarkable French writer, M. Tarde, in an admirable book, Les Lois de l'Imitation. Most of the things we do, we do for no better reason than that our fathers have done them or that our neighbors do them, and the same is true of a larger part than we suspect of what we think. The reason is a good one, because our short life gives us no time for a better, but it is not the best. It does not follow, because we all are compelled to take on faith at second hand most of the rules on which we base our action and our thought, that each of us may not try to set some corner of his world in the order of reason, or that all of us collectively should not aspire to carry reason as far as it will go throughout the whole domain. In regard to the law, it is true, no doubt, that an evolutionist will hesitate to affirm universal validity for his social ideals, or for the principles which he thinks should be embodied in legislation. He is content if he can prove them best for here and now. He may be ready to admit that he knows nothing about an absolute best in the cosmos, and even that he knows next to nothing about a permanent best for men. Still it is true that a body of law is more rational and more civilized when every rule it contains is referred articulately and definitely to an end which it subserves, and when the grounds for desiring that end are stated or are ready to be stated in words.

At present, in very many cases, if we want to know why a rule of law has taken its particular shape, and more or less if we want to know why it exists at all, we go to tradition. We follow it into the Year Books, and perhaps beyond them to the customs of the Salian Franks, and somewhere in the past, in the German forests, in the needs of Norman kings, in the assumptions of a dominant class, in the absence of generalized ideas, we find out the practical motive for what now best is justified by the mere fact of its acceptance and that men are accustomed to it. The rational study of law is still to a large extent the study of history. History must be a part of the study, because without it we cannot know the precise scope of rules which it is our business to know. It is a part of the rational study, because it is the first step toward an enlightened scepticism, that is, towards a deliberate reconsideration of the worth of those rules. When you get the dragon out of his cave on to the plain and in the daylight, you can count his teeth and claws, and see just what is his strength. But to get him out is only the first step. The next is either to kill him, or to tame him and make him a useful animal. For the rational study of the law the black-letter man may be the man of the present, but the man of the future is the man of statistics and the master of economics. It is revolting to have no better reason for a rule of law than that so it was laid down in the time of Henry IV. It is still more revolting if the grounds upon which it was laid down have vanished long since, and the rule simply persists from blind imitation of the past. I am thinking of the technical rule as to trespass *ab initio,* as it is called, which I attempted to explain in a recent Massachusetts case.[3]

Let me take an illustration, which can be stated in a few words, to show how the social end which is aimed at by a rule of law is obscured and only partially attained in consequence of the fact that the rule owes its form to a gradual historical development, instead of being reshaped as a whole, with conscious articulate reference to the end in view. We think it desirable to prevent one man's property being misappropriated by another, and so we make

[3] Commonwealth *v.* Rubin, 165 Mass. 453.

larceny a crime. The evil is the same whether the misappropriation
is made by a man into whose hands the owner has put the property,
or by one who wrongfully takes it away. But primitive law in its
weakness did not get much beyond an effort to prevent violence,
and very naturally made a wrongful taking, a trespass, part of its
definition of the crime. In modern times the judges enlarged the
definition a little by holding that, if the wrongdoer gets possession
by a trick or device, the crime is committed. This really was giving
up the requirement of a trespass, and it would have been more
logical, as well as truer to the present object of the law, to abandon
the requirement altogether. That, however, would have seemed too
bold, and was left to statute. Statutes were passed making embezzlement a crime. But the force of tradition caused the crime of embezzlement to be regarded as so far distinct from larceny that to
this day, in some jurisdictions at least, a slip corner is kept open
for thieves to contend, if indicted for larceny, that they should
have been indicted for embezzlement, and if indicted for embezzlement, that they should have been indicted for larceny, and to
escape on that ground.

Far more fundamental questions still await a better answer than
that we do as our fathers have done. What have we better than a
blind guess to show that the criminal law in its present form does
more good than harm? I do not stop to refer to the effect which it
has had in degrading prisoners and in plunging them further into
crime, or to the question whether fine and imprisonment do not
fall more heavily on a criminal's wife and children than on himself.
I have in mind more far-reaching questions. Does punishment
deter? Do we deal with criminals on proper principles? A modern
school of Continental criminalists plumes itself on the formula, first
suggested, it is said, by Gall, that we must consider the criminal
rather than the crime. The formula does not carry us very far, but
the inquiries which have been started look toward an answer of
my questions based on science for the first time. If the typical criminal is a degenerate, bound to swindle or to murder by as deep-
seated an organic necessity as that which makes the rattlesnake
bite, it is idle to talk of deterring him by the classical method of
imprisonment. He must be got rid of; he cannot be improved, or
frightened out of his structural reaction. If, on the other hand,

crime, like normal human conduct, is mainly a matter of imitation, punishment fairly may be expected to help to keep it out of fashion. The study of criminals has been thought by some well known men of science to sustain the former hypothesis. The statistics of the relative increase of crime in crowded places like large cities, where example has the greatest chance to work, and in less populated parts, where the contagion spreads more slowly, have been used with great force in favor of the latter view. But there is weighty authority for the belief that, however this may be, "not the nature of the crime but the dangerousness of the criminal, constitutes the only reasonable legal criterion to guide the inevitable social reaction against the criminal." [4] . . .

Perhaps I have said enough to show the part which the study of history necessarily plays in the intelligent study of the law as it is to-day. In the teaching of this school and at Cambridge it is in no danger of being undervalued. Mr. Bigelow here and Mr. Ames and Mr. Thayer there have made important contributions which will not be forgotten, and in England the recent history of early English law by Sir Frederick Pollock and Mr. Maitland has lent the subject an almost deceptive charm. We must beware of the pitfall of antiquarianism, and must remember that for our purposes our only interest in the past is for the light it throws upon the present. I look foward to a time when the part played by history in the explanation of dogma shall be very small, and instead of ingenious research we shall spend our energy on a study of the ends sought to be attained and the reasons for desiring them. As a step toward that ideal it seems to me that every lawyer ought to seek an understanding of economics. The present divorce between the schools of political economy and law seems to me an evidence of how much progress in philosophical study still remains to be made. In the present state of political economy, indeed, we come again upon history on a larger scale, but there we are called on to consider and weigh the ends of legislation, the means of attaining them, and the cost. We learn that for everything we have we give up something else, and we are taught to set the advantage we gain

[4] Havelock Ellis, "The Criminal," 41, citing Garafolo. See also Ferri, "Sociologie Criminelle," *passim.* Compare Tarde, "La Philosophie Penale."

against the other advantage we lose, and to know what we are doing when we elect.

There is another study which sometimes is undervalued by the practical minded, for which I wish to say a good word, although I think a good deal of pretty poor stuff goes under that name. I mean the study of what is called jurisprudence. Jurisprudence, as I look at it, is simply law in its most generalized part. Every effort to reduce a case to a rule is an effort of jurisprudence, although the name as used in English is confined to the broadest rules and most fundamental conceptions. One mark of a great lawyer is that he sees the application of the broadest rules. There is a story of a Vermont justice of the peace before whom a suit was brought by one farmer against another for breaking a churn. The justice took time to consider, and then said that he had looked through the statutes and could find nothing about churns, and gave judgment for the defendant. The same state of mind is shown in all our common digests and text-books. Applications of rudimentary rules of contract or tort are tucked away under the head of Railroads or Telegraphs or go to swell treatises on historical subdivisions, such as Shipping or Equity, or are gathered under an arbitrary title which is thought likely to appeal to the practical mind, such as Mercantile Law. If a man goes into law it pays to be a master of it, and to be a master of it means to look straight through all the dramatic incidents and to discern the true basis for prophecy. Therefore, it is well to have an accurate notion of what you mean by law, by a right, by a duty, by malice, intent, and negligence, by ownership, by possession, and so forth. I have in my mind cases in which the highest courts seem to me to have floundered because they had no clear ideas on some of these themes. I have illustrated their importance already. If a further illustration is wished, it may be found by reading the Appendix to Sir James Stephen's Criminal Law on the subject of possession, and then turning to Pollock and Wright's enlightened book. Sir James Stephen is not the only writer whose attempts to analyze legal ideas have been confused by striving for a useless quintessence of all systems, instead of an accurate anatomy of one. The trouble with Austin was that he did not know enough English law. But still it is a prac-

tical advantage to master Austin, and his predecessors, Hobbes
and Bentham, and his worthy successors, Holland and Pollock.
Sir Frederick Pollock's recent little book is touched with the felicity
which marks all his works, and is wholly free from the perverting
influence of Roman models.

The advice of the elders to young men is very apt to be as un-
real as a list of the hundred best books. At least in my day I had
my share of such counsels, and high among the unrealities I place
the recommendation to study the Roman law. I assume that such
advice means more than collecting a few Latin maxims with
which to ornament the discourse,—the purpose for which Lord
Coke recommended Bracton. If that is all that is wanted, the title
"De Regulis Juris Antiqui" can be read in an hour. I assume that, if
it is well to study the Roman law, it is well to study it as a working
system. That means mastering a set of technicalities more difficult
and less understood than our own, and studying another course
of history by which even more than our own the Roman law must
be explained. If anyone doubts me, let him read Keller's "Der
Römische Civil Process und die Actionen," a treatise on the prae-
tor's edict, Muirhead's most interesting "Historical Introduction to
the Private Law of Rome," and, to give him the best chance possible Sohm's admirable "Institutes." No. The way to gain a liberal
view of your subject is not to read something else, but to get to the
bottom of the subject itself. The means of doing that are, in the
first place, to follow the existing body of dogma into its highest
generalizations by the help of jurisprudence; next, to discover from
history how it has come to be what it is; and, finally, so far as you
can, to consider the ends which the several rules seek to accomplish, the reasons why those ends are desired, what is given up to
gain them, and whether they are worth the price. . . .

I have been speaking about the study of the law, and I have said
next to nothing of what commonly is talked about in that connection,—text-books and the case system, and all the machinery
with which a student comes most immediately in contact. Nor
shall I say anything about them. Theory is my subject, not practical
details. The modes of teaching have been improved since my time,

no doubt, but ability and industry will master the raw material with any mode. Theory is the most important part of the dogma of the law, as the architect is the most important man who takes part in the building of a house. The most important improvements of the last twenty-five years are improvements in theory. It is not to be feared as unpractical, for, to the competent, it simply means going to the bottom of the subject. For the incompetent, it sometimes is true, as has been said, that an interest in general ideas means an absence of particular knowledge. I remember in army days reading of a youth who, being examined for the lowest grade and being asked a question about squadron drill, answered that he never had considered the evolutions of less than ten thousand men. But the weak and foolish must be left to their folly. The danger is that the able and practical-minded should look with indifference or distrust upon ideas the connection of which with their business is remote. I heard a story, the other day, of a man who had a valet to whom he paid high wages, subject to deduction for faults. One of his deductions was, "For lack of imagination, five dollars." The lack is not confined to valets. The object of ambition, power, generally presents itself nowadays in the form of money alone. Money is the most immediate form, and is a proper object of desire. "The fortune," said Rachel, "is the measure of the intelligence." That is a good text to waken people out of a fool's paradise. But, as Hegel says,[5] "It is in the end not the appetite, but the opinion, which has to be satisfied." To an imagination of any scope the most far-reaching form of power is not money, it is the command of ideas. If you want great examples read Mr. Leslie Stephen's "History of English Thought in the Eighteenth Century," and see how a hundred years after his death the abstract speculations of Descartes had become a practical force controlling the conduct of men. Read the works of the great German jurists, and see how much more the world is governed to-day by Kant than by Bonaparte. We cannot all be Descartes or Kant, but we all want happiness. And happiness, I am sure from having known many successful men, cannot be won simply by being counsel for great corporations and having an income of fifty thousand dollars. An

[5] Phil. des Rechts, § 190.

intellect great enough to win the prize needs other food besides success. The remoter and more general aspects of the law are those which give it universal interest. It is through them that you not only become a great master in your calling, but connect your subject with the universe and catch an echo of the infinite, a glimpse of its unfathomable process, a hint of the universal law.

Use-Value and Exchange-Value

JOHN R. COMMONS

John Rogers Commons (1862–1945) grew up in a Quaker family in
rural communities in Ohio and Indiana. He did not graduate from
Oberlin College until he was twenty-six years old, at which time he
began his graduate work at Johns Hopkins. He taught sociology at
Indiana and then at Syracuse. Objections to his point of view caused
his job at Syracuse to be abolished and Commons to be dismissed.
He spent five years with the federal government and the National
Civic Federation. In 1904 Richard T. Ely, who had been his professor
at Johns Hopkins, invited him to the University of Wisconsin as
professor of economics. Commons accepted, and stayed there the
rest of his life. Although he was a pioneer in several fields of applied
economics—for instance, he started the first university course in
municipal public utilities and drafted the public-utility law of Wisconsin—he is best known for his work in labor history and labor
economics. Commons reserved most of his systematic theorizing for
his books; the following selection is from his classic *Legal Foundations of Capitalism* first published in 1924 by The Macmillan Company, and is reprinted by permission of The University of Wisconsin
Press.

IN THE YEAR 1872 the Supreme Court of the United States was
called upon, in the Slaughter House Cases,[1] to interpret the meanings of the words Property and Liberty as used in the Constitution
of the United States. The Thirteenth Amendment to the Federal
Constitution, adopted in 1865, prohibited slavery and involuntary

[1] 16 Wall. 36 (1872).

servitude except as punishment for crime, and the Fourteenth Amendment, adopted three years later, prohibited a state from depriving any person of "life, liberty, or property" without "due process of law," and gave to the federal courts jurisdiction. The legislature of Louisiana had granted to a corporation a monopoly to maintain slaughtering places for stock in the city of New Orleans, and had regulated the charges to be made to other butchers who used these facilities. The latter, through their attorneys, contended that the statute deprived them of both their property and their liberty without due process of law. The Supreme Court divided. If the court should hold that property meant exchange-value, then the federal court would take jurisdiction under the Amendments. But if property meant only the use-value of physical things, then the court would not interfere with the legislature of Louisiana. Justice Miller, for the majority, declared that the act was not a deprivation of property or liberty as the terms were used in the Thirteenth and Fourteenth Amendments. The term "liberty," he said, should be construed with reference to the well-known purpose of those Amendments, namely, to establish freedom from slavery or personal servitude. Even conceding that the term "liberty," as popularly used, might mean "civil liberty" or the right to buy and sell, yet that aspect of liberty was not included in the meaning of the term as used in the Amendments. Prior to the adoption of these amendments the liberty of citizens, whether personal, civil or economic, was, for the most part, in the keeping of the states. The Thirteenth and Fourteenth Amendments only transferred from the states to the federal government the protection of such fraction of the total concept of liberty as was comprehended in freedom from personal slavery. All other aspects of liberty were left, as they had been, to the keeping of the states.[2] And as to the meaning of the term "property," as used in the Fourteenth Amendment, he held that the term retained its common-law meaning of physical things held exclusively for one's own use. Property, according to the Fourteenth Amendment, meant use-value, not exchange-value. "Under no construction of that provision that we have ever seen," he said, "can the restraint imposed by the state of Louisiana upon the exercise of their trade by the

[2] 16 Wall. 69-73.

butchers of New Orleans be held to be a deprivation of property within the meaning of that provision." [3] The state of Louisiana had not deprived the butchers of the use-value of their property—it had deprived them of its exchange-value.

The minority of the court, however, contended that the police power (which they admitted, of course, might justly deprive a person of liberty or property for public purposes without compensation), could have been exercised in this case without resorting to a monopoly, by merely regulating all of the butchers alike in the interest of public health, but that the monopoly feature of the law deprived the other butchers of their liberty and property and turned it over to the monopolist. They then went on to define the property and liberty which was thus unjustly taken away, not by a proper exercise of the police power, but by a special privilege granted to the slaughter-house monopolist. A man's "calling," his "occupation," his "trade," his "labor," was property, as well as the physical things which he might own; and "liberty" included his "right of choice," his right to choose a calling, to choose an occupation or trade, to choose the direction in which he would exercise his labor. Justice Bradley, of the minority, for example, declared that the "right to choose one's calling is an essential part of that liberty which it is the object of government to protect; and a calling, when chosen, is a man's property and right. . . . Their right of choice is a portion of their liberty; their occupation is their property." (116, 122.) Justice Field, also of the minority, desired to change the meaning of "slavery" from physical coercion to economic coercion. He said, "A person allowed to pursue only one trade or calling, and only in one locality of the country, would not be, in the strict sense of the term, in a condition of slavery, but probably none would deny that he would be in a condition of servitude. . . . The compulsion which would force him to labor even for his own benefit only in one direction, or in one place, would be almost as oppressive and nearly as great an invasion of his liberty as the compulsion which would force him to labor for the benefit or pleasure of another, and would equally constitute an element of servitude." (90.) Thus Justice Field described slavery as physical coercion and servitude as economic coercion. And

[3] 16 Wall. 81.

Justice Swayne declared, "Property is everything which has exchangeable value, and the right of property includes the power to dispose of it according to the will of the owner. Labor is property, and as such merits protection. The right to make it available is next in importance to the rights of life and liberty." (127.) Thus Justice Swayne defined property as the exchange-value of one's ability to work, and liberty as the right to realize that exchange-value on the labor market.

These minority definitions of liberty and property as exchange-value were unavailing in the Slaughter House Cases. The majority held to the older meaning of use-value. Twelve years later the municipal authorities of New Orleans, acting under a new constitution for the state, granted to another company privileges in conflict with those of the original monopolist, thus infringing upon their exclusive right. This time, therefore, the Slaughter House company was plaintiff against the municipality. The majority of the court now retained its original definition of property and liberty, but now held that not only the original act, as they had contended before, but also this annulling act were a proper exercise of the police power.[4] But Justices Bradley and Field, while concurring in the court's decision, placed it on the grounds of their dissenting opinions in the original Slaughter House Cases, and repeated their earlier views that the original act was itself an unlawful deprivation of liberty and property. In their earlier dissent the minority had not cited any cases where the term *property* had been used in the sense of a trade, occupation, calling, or one's labor, whose value to the owner is in its exchange-value, though they asserted that it *ought* to have that meaning. Thus, in the constitutional sense of the term, they had not been able to controvert Justice Miller's denial that that meaning had ever been given to it. In the later case, however, they suggested the origin of their new definition. Justice Field now stated that this meaning of property was derived from Adam Smith who had said: "The property which every man has in his own labor, as it is the original foundation of all other property, so it is the most sacred and inviolable." [5] And Justice Bradley contented himself with saying, "If a man's right to his calling is prop-

---

[4] Butchers' Union Co. *v.* Crescent City Co., 111 U.S. 746, 751 (1884).
[5] 111 U.S. 746, 757; Smith, *Wealth of Nations*, 1:123 (Cannan ed., 1904).

erty, *as many maintain,* then those who had already adopted the prohibited pursuits in New Orleans, were deprived, by the law in question, of their property, as well as their liberty, without due process of law." [6] Thus the new meanings of property and liberty were found in Adam Smith and the customs of business, and not in the Constitution of the United States.

After the Slaghter House Cases the minority definitions of property and liberty began to creep into the constitutional definitions given by state and federal courts,[7] as indeed was inevitable and proper if the thing itself was thus changing. Finally, in the first Minnesota Rate Case, in 1890,[8] the Supreme Court itself made the transition and changed the definition of property from physical things having only use-value to the exchange-value of anything.

This decision was a partial reversal of the decision of the court in the case of Munn *v.* Illinois in 1876.[9] In the Munn case the Supreme Court had held, agreeably to its holding in the Slaughter House Cases, that when a state legislature reduced the prices which a warehouse company charged for the use of its services the resulting reduction in exchange-value of the business was not a deprivation of property in the sense in which the word was used in the Fourteenth Amendment and therefore was not an act which the federal courts might restrain. It was only a regulation of the "use and enjoyment" of property under the police power of the state. The court went so far as to declare that, if the legislature abused its power, "the people must resort to the polls, not to the courts." [10]

That the state legislatures might possibly abuse their power had been clearly suggested in the decision of the Supreme Court of Illinois in sustaining the act of the Illinois legislature, when the Munn Case was before that court. The Illinois court had held [11] that the authority was not abused in that case by the Illinois legislature, since the property of the owner was not "taken" from him, in

[6] 111 U.S. 765 (my italics).

[7] Powell *v.* Penn., 127 U.S. 678, 684 (1887); Matter of Jacobs, 98 N.Y. 98 (1885); People *v.* Marx, 99 N.Y. 377 (1885); People *v.* Gillson, 109 N.Y. 399 (1888).

[8] Chicago, M. & St. P. Ry. Co. *v.* Minnesota, 134 U.S. 418 (1890).

[9] 94 U.S. 113 (1876).

[10] 94 U.S. 113, 134.

[11] As interpreted by Justice Field, 94 U.S. 139; Munn *v.* People, 69 Ill. 80 (1873).

that he was not deprived of the "title and possession" of the property. In this respect the Illinois court adhered to the primitive definition of property as the mere holding of physical objects for one's own use and enjoyment. The legislature, under the police power of the state, might reduce the charges which a warehouse company had established for its services, but that was not "taking" their property. The owners continued to hold their physical property even though deprived of the power to fix the prices for its use. To this Justice Field had rightly answered, "There is indeed no protection of any value under the constitutional provision which does not extend to the use and income of the property, as well as to its title and possession." [12] For, of course, the title of ownership or the possession of physical property is empty as a business asset if the owner is deprived of his liberty to fix a price on the sale of the product of that property.

But Justice Field in the Munn Case had gone too far. He denied the authority of *both* the legislature *and* the courts to fix the compensation. The majority had only denied the authority of the court to fix it. Fourteen years after Munn v. Illinois this further issue came up in the Minnesota Rate Case,[13] and the petitioners for the railroads asked the court to review the decision in the Munn and similar cases and to restrain the state legislature from fixing finally the prices charged for the use of property. (445.) The court now acceded, and Justice Blatchford, for the majority, wrote, "This power to regulate [police power] is not a power to destroy, and limitation is not the equivalent of confiscation." (456.) And confiscation, or the reasonableness of a rate, "is eminently a question for judicial investigation, requiring due process of law for its determination." (458.) Thus Justice Field's definition of property as the exchange-value of property was approved and, therefore, the protection of that property was brought under the jurisdiction of the federal courts conformably to the Fourteenth Amendment.

But Justice Bradley, who in the Slaughter House Cases had agreed with Justice Field, now again dissented (supported by two other justices) and held that the majority opinion asserted an "assumption of authority on the part of the judiciary which . . . it

[12] 94 U.S. 143.
[13] Chicago, M. & St. P. Ry. Co. *v.* Minnesota, 134 U.S. 418 (1890).

has no right to make." (418, 463.) "If not in terms, yet in effect,"
he said, "the present cases are treated as if the constitutional
prohibition was, that no state shall take private property for public
use without just compensation—and as if it was our duty to judge
of the compensation. But there is no such clause in the Constitution of the United States." (465.) "There was," he said, "in truth,
no deprivation of property in these cases at all. There was merely
a regulation as to the enjoyment of property, made by a strictly
competent authority, in a matter entirely within its jurisdiction."
(466.) In this respect he, like the Illinois court in the Munn Case,
continued to adhere to the primitive definition of property as the
mere exclusive holding of objects for one's own use, a kind of
property that is not taken from the owner unless he is deprived
of its title and possession, for which he is entitled to just compensation.

The majority, however, now held, as they had not held in the
Munn Case, that not merely physical things are objects of property,
but the *expected earning power* of those things is property; and
property is taken from the owner, not merely under the power of
eminent domain which takes *title* and *possession,* but also under
the police power which takes its *exchange-value.* To deprive the
owners of the *exchange-value* of their property is equivalent to
depriving them of their property. Hence, differently from the Munn
Case decision, they now held that, under the Fourteenth Amendment, it is the province of the court, and not the legislature, to
determine the extent to which that "taking" of the value of property might go and yet not pass beyond the point of confiscation.
They thus extended to the exercise of the police power the judicial
authority to ascertain just compensation which the judiciary had
exercised over the power of eminent domain.[14]

Thus the transition in the definition of property from physical
objects to exchange-value was completed. "Title and possession" of
physical property could be taken from its owner for public purposes
under the power of eminent domain, but only on condition that
equivalent value should be paid, such that the owners' assets
should not be reduced; and this equivalent value, or just com-

---

[14] Under the original constitutional provision that no state should take
private property for public use without just compensation.

pensation, is a judicial question. Now it is enlarged to read: The exchange-value of property may be taken from its owners under the police power, but only to the extent that they retain sufficient bargaining power to maintain the same exchange-value that they had, and this also is a judicial question. The definition of property is changed from physical things to the exchange-value of anything, and the federal courts now take jurisdiction.

Evidently, however, the exchange-value of property has no existence if either the owner or expected purchasers are forbidden access to markets where they can sell and buy the property. Hence liberty of access to markets is essential to the definition of exchange-value. This attribute was finally added seven years after the Minnesota Rate Case, in the Allgeyer Case, and the minority definition of liberty in 1872 became the unanimous definition of liberty in 1897.[15] The court now said: "The liberty mentioned in that Amendment [Fourteenth] means not only the right of the citizen to be free from physical restraint of his person, but the term is deemed to embrace the right of the citizen to be free in the enjoyment of all his faculties; to be free to use them in all lawful ways; to live and work where he will; to earn his livelihood by any lawful calling; to pursue any livelihood or avocation, and for that purpose to enter into all contracts which may be proper, necessary, and essential to his carrying out to a successful conclusion the purposes above mentioned. . . . His enjoyment upon terms of equality with all others in similar circumstances of the privilege of pursuing an ordinary calling or trade, and of acquiring, holding, and selling property is an essential part of liberty and property as guaranteed by the Fourteenth Amendment." [16]

Furthermore, while liberty of access to markets on the part of an owner is essential to the exchange-value of property, too much

---

[15] Allgeyer v. Louisiana, 165 U.S. 578, 589 (1897).

[16] Ibid., at 580, 589. This latter sentence was quoted in part from earlier decisions cited above, Powell v. Pennsylvania, 127 U.S. 678, 684 (1888); quoted in 165 U.S. 578, 590. For a discussion of the change in meaning of these terms while the process was going on, in 1891, see Shattuck, C. E., "The True Meaning of the Term 'Liberty' in those clauses in the Federal and State constitutions which protect life, liberty and property." 4 Harv. Law Rev. 365 (1891).

liberty of access on the part of would-be competitors is destructive of that exchange-value. During the past three hundred years this excessive liberty has been restrained by the courts in the long line of cases going under the name of "goodwill" or "unfair competition." Evidently, these decisions of the courts had been designed to protect the exchange-value of property, and now that the definition of property itself had been changed from physical things to the exchange-value of anything, it was an easy step to change the definition of goodwill from "fair competition" to "property." The long-recognized goodwill of a business which had always possessed exchange-value, but which was merely the expected beneficial behavior of other people, now became simply a special case of property. Other courts followed, and the transition from the meaning of property as physical things to that of the most ethereal invisibility was reached in 1902 in a case involving the right to exclusive telephonic communication of news to the daily press by mere word of mouth. The lower court then said, "Property . . . is not, in its modern sense, confined to that which may be touched by the hand, or seen by the eye. What is called tangible property has come to be, in most great enterprises, but the embodiment, physically, of an underlying life—a life that, in its contribution to success, is immeasurably more effective than the mere physical embodiment." [17] And, in 1911, by another lower court, Justice Swayne's definition in 1872 of labor as property became "the right to labor in any calling or profession in the future." [18]

The foregoing cases, it will be noted, have turned on a double meaning of property, and the transition is from one of the meanings to both of the meanings. Property, in the popular ordinary usage, the usage of the old common law and the one adhered to in the Slaughter House Cases and the Munn Case, meant any tangible thing owned. Property, in the later decisions, means any of the expected activities implied with regard to the thing owned, comprehended in the activities of acquiring, using and disposing of the thing. One is Property, the other is Business. The one is property

[17] National Telephone News Co. v. Western Union Tel. Co., 119 Fed. 294, 299 (1902), by Justice Grosscup.
[18] Gleason v. Thaw, 185 Fed. 345, 347 (1911).

in the sense of Things owned, the other is property in the sense of exchange-value of things. One is physical objects, the other is marketable assets.

Thus it is that "corporeal property," in the original meaning of the term, has disappeared, or, rather, has been relegated to what may be described as the internal "economy" of a going concern or a household in the various processes of producing and consuming physical objects, according to what the economists call their "use-value." And, instead of the use-value of corporeal property, the courts are concerned with its exchange-value. This exchange-value is not corporeal—it is behavioristic. It is the market-value expected to be obtained in exchange for the thing in any of the markets where the thing can or might be sold. In the course of time this exchange-value has come to be known as "intangible property," that is, the kind of property whose value depends upon right of access to a commodity market, a labor market, a money market, and so on. Consequently, in conformity with the customs and usages of business, there are only two kinds of property, both of them invisible and behavioristic, since their value depends on ex-pected activities on the commodity and money markets. One of these may technically be distinguishd as "incorporeal property," consisting of debts, credits, bonds, mortgages, in short, of promises to pay; the other may be distinguished as "intangible property," consisting of the exchange-value of anything, whether corporeal property or incorporeal property or even intangible property. The short name for intangible property is *assets*. Assets is the expected exchange-value of anything, whether it be one's reputation, one's horse, house or land, one's ability to work, one's goodwill, patent right, good credit, stocks, bonds or bank deposit. In short, intangi-ble property is anything that enables one to obtain from others an income in the process of buying and selling, borrowing and lending, hiring and hiring out, renting and leasing, in any of the transactions of modern business. We shall identify these two classes of property as "encumbrances" and "opportunities." Encumbrances are in-corporeal property, that is, promises to pay, enforced by govern-ment; opportunities are intangible property, that is, accessibility to markets, also enforced by government.

Going back, therefore, to the common-law meaning of property as physical things held for the owner's use, we find that what property really signified, even in that original sense, was not the physical thing itself but the expected "uses" of the thing, that is, various activities regarding the thing. These uses, or activities, arose from the producing and consuming power of a person in control of, or working with, the thing. The legal terms carry this futuristic, behavioristic meaning. The legal term *use* is said to have been derived from the Latin *opus,* meaning work or working, through the Anglo-French *oeps* and the Old French *oes.*[19] It means the work a person can do with a thing, his behavior respecting the thing. Thus it differs from the economic term *utility,* which is derived from the Latin *usus,* through the French *utilité,* and means the satisfaction a person gets in using a thing. Use is behavior. Utility is feeling. The early feudal grants of land to tenants were granted *ad opus*—that is, "to the use" of the tenant in production and consumption. Then when property began to yield exchange-value as well as use-value, the term "uses" was simply enlarged by the courts to include it. It now means both the expected use-values of production and consumption and the expected exchange-values of selling and buying.

The difference is unimportant in the law of private property. In fact, the term *uses* has a social meaning and a business meaning. Socially it means what we understand by producing and consuming things; that is, increasing the supply and enjoyment of things. But in the business sense it means also acquiring and disposing of the thing in transactions with other people. This explains the easy transition from the common-law meaning of property as physical things, valuable to owners on account of the expected physical uses of production and consumption, to the business-law meaning of property as *assets,* valuable to owners on account of their expected bargaining uses as purchasing power in buying and selling.

The common-law and popular notion of property as physical things is, therefore, but an elliptical statement of what common-sense can take for granted without the pedantry of explaining every time that what is meant by property is the *uses* and not the thing.

[19] Pollock, F., *Principles of Contract,* 5 (9th ed., 1921); 3 *Law. Quar. Rev.,* 115 (1887); Bouvier's *Law Dictionary,* title "Use."

The trouble is that, by using this common-sense notion of uses, not only the courts and business men, but also theoretical economists, pass over from the significance of "uses" in the sense of producing an increase in the supply of goods, to its exact opposite meaning in the business sense of an increase in the power of owners to command goods from other persons in exchange. The one is *producing power* which *increases* the supply of goods in order to increase the quantity of use-values; the other is *bargaining power* which *restricts* the supply of goods in proportion to demand, in order to increase or maintain their exchange-value. Bargaining power is the willful *restriction* of supply in proportion to demand in order to maintain or enlarge the value of business assets; but producing power is the willing *increase* of supply in order to enlarge the wealth of nations.

Hence the transition in the meaning of property from the use-value to the exchange-value of things, and therefore from the producing power that increases use-values to the bargaining power that increases exchange-values, is more than a transition—it is a reversal. The reversal was not at first important when business was small and weak—it becomes important when Capitalism rules the world.

The transition in meanings of property and liberty applies to agriculture as well as manufactures, commerce and transportation, and to individuals, partnerships and associations as well as corporations. Farming has become a going business, or a bankrupt business, like other businesses. The isolated, colonial, or frontier farmer might produce and consume things, attentive only to their use-value, but the modern farmer lives by producing "social-use-values" and buying other social-use-values produced and sold by other business men. In this way he also "produces" exchange-value, that is, assets. He farms for sale, not for use, and while he has the doubtful alternative of falling back on his own natural resources if he cannot sell his products, yet his farm and crops are valuable because they are business assets, that is, exchange-values, while his liabilities are his debts and his taxes, all of them measured by his expectations and realizations on the commodity markets and money markets, in terms of exchange-value or price.

This, we take it, is the substance of Capitalism distinguished from the Feudalism or Colonialism which it displaced—production for the use of others and acquisition for the use of self, such that the meaning of property and liberty spreads out from the expected uses of production and consumption to expected transactions on the markets where one's assets and liabilities are determined by the ups and downs of prices. And this is, in substance, the change in the meanings of Property and Liberty, from the Slaughter House Cases in 1872 to the Allgeyer Case in 1897, a change from the use-value of physical things to the exchange-values of anything.

The Significance of the Frontier in American History

FREDERICK JACKSON TURNER

Frederick Jackson Turner was born in 1861 at Portage, Wisconsin, and during his youth and early manhood he watched that area change from a primitive community on the farming frontier into a settled agricultural region. Awarded his Ph.D. by Johns Hopkins in 1890, Turner returned to the University of Wisconsin where he had done his undergraduate work. In 1892 he became professor of American history, and the following year, at a meeting of the American Historical Association during the Columbian Exposition in Chicago, he read his famous essay, "The Significance of the Frontier in American History." It is reprinted here from the *Report of the American Historical Association* (1893). The rest of Turner's career, at Wisconsin until 1910, then at Harvard until 1924, was spent in elaborating and particularizing the ideas presented here. He died in 1932.

IN A RECENT bulletin of the Superintendent of the Census for 1890 appear these significant words: "Up to and including 1880 the country had a frontier of settlement, but at present the unsettled area has been so broken into by isolated bodies of settlement that there can hardly be said to be a frontier line. In the discussion of its extent, its westward movement, etc., it can not, therefore, any longer have a place in the census reports." This brief official statement marks the closing of a great historic movement. Up to our own day American history has been in a large degree the history of the colonization of the Great West. The existence of an area of free land, its continuous recession, and the advance of American settlement westward, explain American development.

Behind institutions, behind constitutional forms and modifications, lie the vital forces that call these organs into life and shape them to meet changing conditions. The peculiarity of American institutions is the fact that they have been compelled to adapt themselves to the changes of an expanding people—to the changes involved in crossing a continent, in winning a wilderness, and in developing at each area of this progress out of the primitive economic and political conditions of the frontier into the complexity of city life. Said Calhoun in 1817, "We are great, and rapidly—I was about to say fearfully—growing!" [1] So saying, he touched the distinguishing feature of American life. All peoples show development; the germ theory of politics has been sufficiently emphasized. In the case of most nations, however, the development has occurred in a limited area; and if the nation has expanded, it has met other growing peoples whom it has conquered. But in the case of the United States we have a different phenomenon. Limiting our attention to the Atlantic coast, we have the familiar phenomenon of the evolution of institutions in a limited area, such as the rise of representative government; the differentiation of simple colonial governments into complex organs; the progress from primitive industrial society, without division of labor, up to manufacturing civilization. But we have in addition to this a recurrence of the process of evolution in each western area reached in the process of expansion. Thus American development has exhibited not merely advance along a single line, but a return to primitive conditions on a continually advancing frontier line, and a new development for that area. American social development has been continually beginning over again on the frontier. This perennial rebirth, this fluidity of American life, this expansion westward with its new opportunities, its continuous touch with the simplicity of primitive society, furnish the forces dominating American character. The true point of view in the history of this nation is not the Atlantic coast, it is the great West. Even the slavery struggle, which is made so exclusive an object of attention by writers like

[1] Abridgment of Debates of Congress, v, p. 706.

Professor von Holst, occupies its important place in American history because of its relation to westward expansion.

In this advance, the frontier is the outer edge of the wave—the meeting point between savagery and civilization. Much has been written about the frontier from the point of view of border warfare and the chase, but as a field for the serious study of the economist and the historian it has been neglected.

The American frontier is sharply distinguished from the European frontier—a fortified boundary line running through dense populations. The most significant thing about the American frontier is, that it lies at the hither edge of free land. In the census reports it is treated as the margin of that settlement which has a density of two or more to the square mile. The term is an elastic one, and for our purposes does not need sharp definition. We shall consider the whole frontier belt, including the Indian country and the outer margin of the "settled area" of the census reports. This paper will make no attempt to treat the subject exhaustively; its aim is simply to call attention to the frontier as a fertile field for investigation, and to suggest some of the problems which arise in connection with it.

In the settlement of America we have to observe how European life entered the continent, and how America modified and developed that life and reacted on Europe. Our early history is the study of European germs developing in an American environment. Too exclusive attention has been paid by institutional students to the Germanic origins, too little to the American factors. The frontier is the line of most rapid and effective Americanization. The wilderness masters the colonist. It finds him a European in dress, industries, tools, modes of travel, and thought. It takes him from the railroad car and puts him in the birch canoe. It strips off the garments of civilization and arrays him in the hunting shirt and the moccasin. It puts him in the log cabin of the Cherokee and Iroquois and runs an Indian palisade around him. Before long he has gone to planting Indian corn and plowing with a sharp stick; he shouts the war cry and takes the scalp in orthodox Indian fashion. In short, at the frontier the environment is at first too strong for the man. He must accept the conditions which it furnishes, or perish, and so he fits himself into the Indian clearings and follows the Indian trails. Little by little he transforms the wilderness, but the outcome is not the old Europe, not simply the development of Germanic germs, any more than the first phenomenon was a case of reversion to the Germanic mark. The fact is, that here is a new product that is American. At first, the frontier was the Atlantic coast. It was the frontier of Europe in a very real sense. Moving westward, the frontier became more and more American. As successive terminal moraines result from successive glaciations, so each frontier leaves its traces behind it, and when it becomes a settled area the region still partakes of the frontier characteristics. Thus the advance of the frontier has meant a steady movement away from the influence of Europe, a steady growth of independence on American lines. And to study this advance, the men who grew up under these conditions, and the political, economic, and social results of it, is to study the really American part of our history.

In the course of the seventeenth century the frontier was advanced up the Atlantic river courses, just beyond the "fall line," and the tidewater region became the settled area. In the first half of the eighteenth century another advance occurred. Traders followed the Delaware and Shawnese Indians to the Ohio as early as the end of the first quarter of the century.[2] Gov. Spotswood, of Virginia, made an expedition in 1714 across the Blue Ridge. The end of the first quarter of the century saw the advance of the Scotch-Irish and the Palatine Germans up the Shenandoah Valley into the western part of Virginia, and along the Piedmont region of the Carolinas.[3] The Germans in New York pushed the frontier of settlement up the Mohawk to German Flats.[4] In Pennsylvania the town of Bedford indicates the line of settlement. Settlements on New River, a branch of the Great Kanawha, and on the

[2] Bancroft (1860 ed.), iii, pp. 344, 345, citing Logan MSS.; [Mitchell] "Contest in America," etc. (1752), p. 237.

[3] Kercheval, "History of the Valley"; Bernheim, "German Settlements in the Carolinas"; Winsor, "Narrative and Critical History of America," v, p. 304; Colonial Records of North Carolina, iv, p. xx; Weston, "Documents Connected with the History of South Carolina," p. 82; Ellis and Evans, "History of Lancaster County, Pa.," chs. iii, xxvi.

[4] Parkman, "Pontiac," ii; Griffis, "Sir William Johnson," p. 6; Simms's "Frontiersmen of New York."

sources of the Yadkin and French Broad.[5] The King attempted
to arrest the advance by his proclamation of 1763,[6] forbidding settlements beyond the sources of the rivers flowing into the Atlantic;
but in vain. In the period of the Revolution the frontier crossed the
Alleghanies into Kentucky and Tennessee, and the upper waters of
the Ohio were settled.[7] When the first census was taken in 1790,
the continuous settled area was bounded by a line which ran near
the coast of Maine, and included New England except a portion
of Vermont and New Hampshire, New York along the Hudson
and up the Mohawk about Schenectady, eastern and southern
Pennsylvania, Virginia well across the Shenandoah Valley, and the
Carolinas and eastern Georgia.[8] Beyond this region of continuous
settlement were the small settled areas of Kentucky and Tennessee,
and the Ohio, with the mountains intervening between them and
the Atlantic area, thus giving a new and important character to the
frontier. The isolation of the region increased its peculiarly American tendencies, and the need of transportation facilities to connect
it with the East called out important schemes of internal improvement, which will be noted farther on. The "West," as a self-con-
scious section, began to evolve.

From decade to decade distinct advances of the frontier occurred. By the census of 1820[9] the settled area included Ohio,
southern Indiana and Illinois, southeastern Missouri, and about

[5] Monette, "Mississippi Valley," i, p. 311.

[6] Wis. Hist. Cols., xi, p. 50; Hinsdale, "Old Northwest," p. 121; Burke,
"Oration on Conciliation," Works (1872 ed.), i, p. 473.

[7] Roosevelt, "Winning of the West," and citations there given; Cutler's
"Life of Cutler."

[8] Scribner's Statistical Atlas, xxxviii, pl. 13; McMaster, "Hist. of People
of U.S.," i, pp. 4, 60, 61; Imlay and Filson, "Western Territory of America"
(London, 1793); Rochefoucault-Liancourt, "Travels Through the United
States of North America" (London, 1799); Michaux's "Journal," in Proceedings American Philosophical Society, xxvi, No. 129; Forman, "Narrative
of a Journey Down the Ohio and Mississippi in 1780-'90" (Cincinnati,
1888); Bartram, "Travels Through North Carolina," etc. (London, 1792);
Pope, "Tour Through the Southern and Western Territories," etc. (Rich-
mond, 1792); Weld, "Travels Through the States of North America" (London, 1799); Baily, "Journal of a Tour in the Unsettled States of North
America, 1796-'97" (London, 1856); Pennsylvania Magazine of History,
July, 1886; Winsor, "Narrative and Critical History of America," vii, pp.
491, 492, citations.

[9] Scribner's Statistical Atlas, xxxix.

one-half of Louisiana. This settled area had surrounded Indian areas, and the management of these tribes became an object of political concern. The frontier region of the time lay along the Great Lakes, where Astor's American Fur Company operated in the Indian trade,[10] and beyond the Mississippi, where Indian traders extended their activity even to the Rocky Mountains; Florida also furnished frontier conditions. The Mississippi River region was the scene of typical frontier settlements.[11]

The rising steam navigation[12] on western waters, the opening of the Erie Canal, and the westward extension of cotton[13] culture added five frontier states to the Union in this period. Grund, writing in 1836, declares: "It appears then that the universal disposition of Americans to emigrate to the western wilderness, in order to enlarge their dominion over inanimate nature, is the actual result of an expansive power which is inherent in them, and which by continually agitating all classes of society is constantly throwing a large portion of the whole population on the extreme confines of the State, in order to gain space for its development. Hardly is a new State or Territory formed before the same principle manifests itself again and gives rise to a further emigration; and so is it destined to go on until a physical barrier must finally obstruct its progress." [14]

[10] Turner, "Character and Influence of the Indian Trade in Wisconsin" (Johns Hopkins University Studies, Series ix), pp. 61 ff.

[11] Monette, "History of the Mississippi Valley," ii; Flint, "Travels and Residence in Mississippi"; Flint, "Geography and History of the Western States"; "Abridgment of Debates of Congress," vii, pp. 397, 398, 404; Holmes, "Account of the U.S."; Kingdom, "America and the British Colonies" (London, 1820); Grund, "Americans," ii, chs. i, iii, vi (although writing in 1836, he treats of conditions that grew out of western advance from the era of 1820 to that time); Peck, "Guide for Emigrants" (Boston, 1831); Darby, "Emigrants' Guide to Western and Southwestern States and Territories"; Dana, "Geographical Sketches in the Western Country"; Kinzie, "Waubun"; Keating, "Narrative of Long's Expedition"; Schoolcraft, "Discovery of the Sources of the Mississippi River," "Travels in the Central Portions of the Mississippi Valley," and "Lead Mines of the Missouri"; Andreas, "History of Illinois," i, 86-99; Hurlbut, "Chicago Antiquities"; McKenney, "Tour to the Lakes"; Thomas, "Travels Through the Western Country," etc. (Auburn, N.Y., 1819).

[12] Darby, "Emigrants' Guide," pp. 272 ff.; Benton, "Abridgment of Debates," vii, p. 397.

[13] DeBow's *Review*, iv, p. 254; xvii, p. 428.

[14] Grund, "Americans," ii, p. 8.

In the middle of this century the line indicated by the present eastern boundary of Indian Territory, Nebraska, and Kansas marked the frontier of the Indian country.[15] Minnesota and Wisconsin still exhibited frontier conditions,[16] but the distinctive frontier of the period is found in California, where the gold discoveries had sent a sudden tide of adventurous miners, and in Oregon, and the settlements in Utah.[17] As the frontier had leaped over the Alleghanies, so now it skipped the Great Plains and the Rocky Mountains; and in the same way that the advance of the frontiersmen beyond the Alleghanies had caused the rise of important questions of transportation and internal improvement, so now the settlers beyond the Rocky Mountains needed means of communication with the East, and in the furnishing of these arose the settlement of the Great Plains and the development of still another kind of frontier life. Railroads, fostered by land grants, sent an increasing tide of immigrants into the far West. The United States Army fought a series of Indian wars in Minnesota, Dakota, and the Indian Territory.

By 1880 the settled area had been pushed into northern Michigan, Wisconsin, and Minnesota, along Dakota rivers, and in the Black Hills region, and was ascending the rivers of Kansas and

[15] Peck, "New Guide to the West" (Cincinnati, 1848), ch. iv; Parkman, "Oregon Trail"; Hall, "The West" (Cincinnati, 1848); Pierce, "Incidents of Western Travel"; Murray, "Travels in North America"; Lloyd, "Steamboat Directory" (Cincinnati, 1856); "Forty Days in a Western Hotel" (Chicago), in *Putnam's Magazine*, December, 1894; Mackay, "The Western World," ii, ch. ii, iii; Meeker, "Life in the West"; Bogen, "German in America" (Boston, 1851); Olmstead, "Texas Journey"; Greeley, "Recollections of a Busy Life"; Schouler, "History of the United States," v, 261-267; Peyton, "Over the Alleghanies and Across the Prairies" (London, 1870); Loughborough, "The Pacific Telegraph and Railway" (St. Louis, 1849); Whitney, "Project for a Railroad to the Pacific" (New York, 1849); Peyton, "Suggestions on Railroad Communication with the Pacific, and the Trade of China and the Indian Islands"; Benton, "Highway to the Pacific" (a speech delivered in the U.S. Senate, December 16, 1850).

[16] A writer in *The Home Missionary* (1850), p. 239, reporting Wisconsin conditions, exclaims: "Think of this, people of the enlightened East. What an examle, to come from the very frontiers of civilization!" But one of the missionaries writes: "In a few years Wisconsin will no longer be considered as the West, or as an outpost of civilization, any more than western New York, or the Western Reserve."

[17] Bancroft (H. H.), "History of California," "History of Oregon," and "Popular Tribunals"; Shinn, "Mining Camps."

Nebraska. The development of mines in Colorado had drawn isolated frontier settlements into that region, and Montana and Idaho were receiving settlers. The frontier was found in these mining camps and the ranches of the Great Plains. The superintendent of the census for 1890 reports, as previously stated, that the settlements of the West lie so scattered over the region that there can no longer be said to be a frontier line.

In these successive frontiers we find natural boundary lines which have served to mark and to affect the characteristics of the frontiers, namely: The "fall line"; the Alleghany Mountains; the Mississippi; the Missouri, where its direction approximates north and south; the line of the arid lands, approximately the ninety-ninth meridian; and the Rocky Mountains. The fall line marked the frontier of the seventeenth century; the Alleghanies that of the eighteenth; the Mississippi that of the first quarter of the nineteenth; the Missouri that of the middle of this century (omitting the California movement); and the belt of the Rocky Mountains and the arid tract, the present frontier. Each was won by a series of Indian wars.

At the Atlantic frontier one can study the germs of processes repeated at each successive frontier. We have the complex European life sharply precipitated by the wilderness into the simplicity of primitive conditions. The first frontier had to meet its Indian question, its question of the disposition of the public domain, of the means of intercourse with older settlements, of the extension of political organization, of religious and educational activity. And the settlement of these and similar questions for one frontier served as a guide for the next. The American student needs not to go to the "prim little townships of Sleswick" for illustrations of the law of continuity and development. For example, he may study the origin of our land policies in the colonial land policy; he may see how the system grew by adapting the statutes to the customs of the successive frontiers.[18] He may see how the mining experience in the lead regions of Wisconsin, Illinois, and Iowa was applied to the mining laws of the Rockies,[19] and how our Indian policy has

[18] See the suggestive paper by Prof. Jesse Macy, "The Institutional Beginnings of a Western State."
[19] Shinn, "Mining Camps."

been a series of experimentations on successive frontiers. Each
tier of new States has found in the older ones material for its constitutions.[20] Each frontier has made similar contributions to American character, as will be discussed farther on.

But with all these similarities there are essential differences,
due to the place element and the time element. It is evident that
the farming frontier of the Mississippi Valley presents different
conditions from the mining frontier of the Rocky Mountains. The
frontier reached by the Pacific Railroad, surveyed into rectangles,
guarded by the United States Army, and recruited by the daily immigrant ship, moves forward at a swifter pace and in a different
way than the frontier reached by the birch canoe or the pack horse.
The geologist traces patiently the shores of ancient seas, maps their
areas, and compares the older and the newer. It would be a work
worth the historian's labors to mark these various frontiers and in
detail compare one with another. Not only would there result a
more adequate conception of American development and characteristics, but invaluable additions would be made to the history
of society.

Loria,[21] the Italian economist, has urged the study of colonial
life as an aid in understanding the stages of European development, affirming that colonial settlement is for economic science
what the mountain is for geology, bringing to light primitive
stratifications. "America," he says, "has the key to the historical
enigma which Europe has sought for centuries in vain, and the
land which has no history reveals luminously the course of universal history." There is much truth in this. The United States
lies like a huge page in the history of society. Line by line as we
read this continental page from West to East we find the record of
social evolution. It begins with the Indian and the hunter; it goes
on to tell of the disintegration of savagery by the entrance of the
trader, the pathfinder of civilization; we read the annals of the
pastoral stage in ranch life; the exploitation of the soil by the
raising of unrotated crops of corn and wheat in sparsely settled

[20] Compare Thorpe, in *Annals American Academy of Political and Social
Science,* September, 1891; Bryce, "American Commonwealth" (1888), ii,
p. 689.

[21] Loria, Analisi della Proprieta Capitalista, ii, p. 15.

farming communities; the intensive culture of the denser farm settlement; and finally the manufacturing organization with city and factory system.[22] This page is familiar to the student of census statistics, but how little of it has been used by our historians. Particularly in eastern States this page is a palimpsest. What is now a manufacturing State was in an earlier decade an area of intensive farming. Earlier yet it had been a wheat area, and still earlier the "range" had attracted the cattle-herder. Thus Wisconsin, now developing manufacture, is a State with varied agricultural interests. But earlier it was given over to almost exclusive grain-raising, like North Dakota at the present time.

Each of these areas has had an influence in our economic and political history; the evolution of each into a higher stage has worked political transformations. But what constitutional historian has made any adequate attempt to interpret political facts by the light of these social areas and changes? [23]

The Atlantic frontier was compounded of fisherman, fur-trader, miner, cattle-raiser, and farmer. Excepting the fisherman, each type of industry was on the march toward the West, impelled by an irresistible attraction. Each passed in successive waves across the continent. Stand at Cumberland Gap and watch the procession of civilization, marching single file—the buffalo following the trail to the salt springs, the Indian, the fur-trader and hunter, the cattle-raiser, the pioneer farmer—and the frontier has passed by. Stand at South Pass in the Rockies a century later and see the same procession with wider intervals between. The unequal rate of advance compels us to distinguish the frontier into the trader's frontier, the rancher's frontier, or the miner's frontier, and the farmer's frontier. When the mines and the cow pens were still near the fall line the traders' pack trains were tinkling across the Alleghanies, and the French on the Great Lakes were fortifying their posts, alarmed by the British trader's birch canoe. When the

[22] Compare "Observations on the North American Land Company," London, 1796, pp. xv, 144; Logan, "History of Upper South Carolina," i, pp. 149–151; Turner, "Character and Influence of Indian Trade in Wisconsin," p. 18; Peck, "New Guide for Emigrants" (Boston, 1837), ch. iv; "Compendium Eleventh Census," i, p. xl.

[23] See pp. 111, 112, 114, *post*, for illustrations of the political accompaniments of changed industrial conditions.

trappers scaled the Rockies, the farmer was still near the mouth of the Missouri.

Why was it that the Indian trader passed so rapidly across the continent? What effects followed from the trader's frontier? The trade was coeval with American discovery. The Norsemen, Vespuccius, Verrazani, Hudson, John Smith, all trafficked for furs. The Plymouth pilgrims settled in Indian cornfields, and their first return cargo was of beaver and lumber. The records of the various New England colonies show how steadily exploration was carried into the wilderness by this trade. What is true for New England is, as would be expected, even plainer for the rest of the colonies. All along the coast from Maine to Georgia the Indian trade opened up the river courses. Steadily the trader passed westward, utilizing the older lines of French trade. The Ohio, the Great Lakes, the Mississippi, the Missouri, and the Platte, the lines of western advance, were ascended by traders. They found the passes in the Rocky Mountains and guided Lewis and Clark,[24] Frémont, and Bidwell. The explanation of the rapidity of this advance is connected with the effects of the trader on the Indian. The trading post left the unarmed tribes at the mercy of those that had purchased fire-arms—a truth which the Iroquois Indians wrote in blood, and so the remote and unvisited tribes gave eager welcome to the trader. "The savages," wrote La Salle, "take better care of us French than of their own children; from us only can they get guns and goods." This accounts for the trader's power and the rapidity of his advance. Thus the disintegrating forces of civilization entered the wilderness. Every river valley and Indian trail became a fissure in Indian society, and so that society became honeycombed. Long before the pioneer farmer appeared on the scene, primitive Indian life had passed away. The farmers met Indians armed with guns. The trading frontier, while steadily undermining Indian power by making the tribes ultimately dependent on the whites, yet, through its sale of guns, gave to the Indians increased power of resistance to the farming frontier. French colonization was dominated by its trading frontier; English colonization by its farming frontier. There was an antagonism between

[24] But Lewis and Clark were the first to explore the route from the Missouri to the Columbia.

the two frontiers as between the two nations. Said Duquesne to the Iroquois, "Are you ignorant of the difference between the king of England and the king of France? Go see the forts that our king has established and you will see that you can still hunt under their very walls. They have been placed for your advantage in places which you frequent. The English, on the contrary, are no sooner in possession of a place than the game is driven away. The forest falls before them as they advance, and the soil is laid bare so that you can scarce find the wherewithal to erect a shelter for the night."

And yet, in spite of this opposition of the interests of the trader and the farmer, the Indian trade pioneered the way for civilization. The buffalo trail became the Indian trail, and this became the trader's "trace"; the trails widened into roads, and the roads into turnpikes, and these in turn were transformed into railroads. The same origin can be shown for the railroads of the South, the far West, and the Dominion of Canada.[25] The trading posts reached by these trails were on the sites of Indian villages which had been placed in positions suggested by nature; and these trading posts, situated so as to command the water systems of the country, have grown into such cities as Albany, Pittsburgh, Detroit, Chicago, St. Louis, Council Bluffs, and Kansas City. Thus civilization in America has followed the arteries made by geology, pouring an even richer tide through them, until at last the slender paths of aboriginal intercourse have been broadened and interwoven into the complex mazes of modern commercial lines; the wilderness has been interpenetrated by lines of civilization growing ever more numerous. It is like the steady growth of a complex nervous system for the originally simple, inert continent. If one would understand why we are today one nation, rather than a collection of isolated states, he must study this economic and social consolidation of the country. In this progress from savage conditions lie topics for the evolutionist.[26]

The effect of the Indian frontier as a consolidating agent in

[25] "Narrative and Critical History of America," viii, p. 10; Sparks' "Washington Works," ix, pp. 303, 327; Logan, "History of Upper South Carolina," i; McDonald, "Life of Kenton," p. 72; Cong. Record, xxiii, p. 57.

[26] On the effect of the fur trade in opening the routes of migration, see the author's "Character and Influence of the Indian Trade in Wisconsin."

our history is important. From the close of the seventeenth century various intercolonial congresses have been called to treat with Indians and establish common measures of defense. Particularism was strongest in colonies with no Indian frontier. This frontier stretched along the western border like a cord of union. The Indian was a common danger, demanding united action. Most celebrated of these conferences was the Albany congress of 1754, called to treat with the Six Nations, and to consider plans of union. Even a cursory reading of the plan proposed by the congress reveals the importance of the frontier. The powers of the general council and the officers were, chiefly, the determination of peace and war with the Indians, the regulation of Indian trade, the purchase of Indian lands, and the creation and government of new settlements as a security against the Indians. It is evident that the unifying tendencies of the Revolutionary period were facilitated by the previous coöperation in the regulation of the frontier. In this connection may be mentioned the importance of the frontier, from that day to this, as a military training school, keeping alive the power of resistance to aggression, and developing the stalwart and rugged qualities of the frontiersman.

It would not be possible in the limits of this paper to trace the other frontiers across the continent. Travelers of the eighteenth century found the "cowpens" among the canebrakes and peavine pastures of the South, and the "cow drivers" took their droves to Charleston, Philadelphia, and New York.[27] Travelers at the close of the War of 1812 met droves of more than a thousand cattle and swine from the interior of Ohio going to Pennsylvania to fatten for the Philadelphia market.[28] The ranges of the Great Plains, with ranch and cowboy and nomadic life, are things of yesterday and of today. The experience of the Carolina cowpens guided the ranchers of Texas. One element favoring the rapid extension of the rancher's frontier is the fact that in a remote country lacking transportation facilities the product must be in small bulk, or must be able to transport itself, and the cattle-raiser could easily drive his product to market. The effect of these great

[27] Lodge, "English Colonies," p. 152 and citations; Logan, "Hist. of Upper South Carolina," i, p. 151.
[28] Flint, "Recollections," p. 9.

ranches on the subsequent agrarian history of the localities in which they existed should be studied.

The maps of the census reports show an uneven advance of the farmer's frontier, with tongues of settlement pushed forward and with indentations of wilderness. In part this is due to Indian resistance, in part to the location of river valleys and passes, in part to the unequal force of the centers of frontier attraction. Among the important centers of attraction may be mentioned the following: fertile and favorably situated soils, salt springs, mines, and army posts.

The frontier army post, serving to protect the settlers from the Indians, has also acted as a wedge to open the Indian country, and has been a nucleus for settlement.[29] In this connection mention should also be made of the government military and exploring expeditions in determining the lines of settlement. But all the more important expeditions were greatly indebted to the earliest pathmakers, the Indian guides, the traders and trappers, and the French voyageurs, who were inevitable parts of governmental expeditions from the days of Lewis and Clark.[30] Each expedition was an epitome of the previous factors in western advance.

In an interesting monograph, Victor Hehn[31] has traced the effect of salt upon early European development, and has pointed out how it affected the lines of settlement and the form of administration. A similar study might be made for the salt springs of the United States. The early settlers were tied to the coast by the need of salt, without which they could not preserve their meats or live in comfort. Writing in 1752, Bishop Spangenburg says of a colony for which he was seeking lands in North Carolina, "They will require salt & other necessaries which they can neither manufacture nor raise. Either they must go to Charleston, which is 300 miles distant . . . Or else they must go to Boling's Point in V^a on a branch of the James & is also 300 miles from here . . . Or else they must go down the Roanoke—I know not how many miles—where salt is brought up from the Cape Fear."[32] This

[29] See Monette, "Mississippi Valley," i, p. 344.

[30] Coues' "Lewis and Clark's Expedition," i, pp. 2, 253-259; Benton, in Cong. Record, xxiii, p. 57.

[31] Hehn, *Das Salz* (Berlin, 1873).

[32] Col. Records of N.C., v, p. 3.

may serve as a typical illustration. An annual pilgrimage to the coast for salt thus became essential. Taking flocks or furs and ginseng root, the early settlers sent their pack trains after seeding time each year to the coast.[33] This proved to be an important educational influence, since it was almost the only way in which the pioneer learned what was going on in the East. But when discovery was made of the salt springs of the Kanawha and the Holston and Kentucky and central New York, the West began to be freed from dependence on the coast. It was in part the effect of finding these salt springs that enabled settlement to cross the mountains.

From the time the mountains rose between the pioneer and the seaboard, a new order of Americanism arose. The West and the East began to get out of touch of each other. The settlements from the sea to the mountains kept connection with the rear and had a certain solidarity. But the over-mountain men grew more and more independent. The East took a narrow view of American advance, and nearly lost these men. Kentucky and Tennessee history bears abundant witness to the truth of this statement. The East began to try to hedge and limit westward expansion. Though Webster could declare that there were no Alleghanies in his politics, yet in politics in general they were a very solid factor.

The exploitation of the beasts took hunter and trader to the west, the exploitation of the grasses took the rancher west, and the exploitation of the virgin soil of the river valleys and prairies attracted the farmer. Good soils have been the most continuous attraction to the farmer's frontier. The land hunger of the Virginians drew them down the rivers into Carolina in early colonial days; the search for soils took the Massachusetts men to Pennsylvania and to New York. As the eastern lands were taken up, migration flowed across them to the west. Daniel Boone, the great backwoodsman, who combined the occupations of hunter, trader, cattle-raiser, farmer, and surveyor—learning, probably from the traders, of the fertility of the lands on the upper Yadkin,

[33] Findley, "History of the Insurrection in the Four Western Counties of Pennsylvania in the Year 1794" (Philadelphia, 1796), p. 35.

where the traders were wont to rest as they took their way to the
Indians—left his Pennsylvania home with his father and passed
down the Great Valley road to that stream. Learning from a trader
of the game and rich pastures of Kentucky, he pioneered the way
for the farmers to that region. Thence he passed to the frontier of
Missouri, where his settlement was long a landmark on the frontier.
Here again he helped to open the way for civilization, finding salt
licks, and trails, and land. His son was among the earliest trappers
in the passes of the Rocky Mountains, and his party are said to
have been the first to camp on the present site of Denver. His
grandson, Col. A. J. Boone of Colorado, was a power among the
Indians of the Rocky Mountains, and was appointed an agent by
the Government. Kit Carson's mother was a Boone.[34] Thus this
family epitomizes the backwoodsman's advance across the continent.

The farmer's advance came in a distinct series of waves. In
Peck's New Guide to the West, published in Boston in 1837,
occurs this suggestive passage:

Generally, in all the western settlements, three classes, like the waves
of the ocean, have rolled one after the other. First comes the pioneer,
who depends for the subsistence of his family chiefly upon the natural
growth of vegetation, called the "range," and the proceeds of hunting.
His implements of agriculture are rude, chiefly of his own make, and
his efforts directed mainly to a crop of corn and a "truck patch." The
last is a rude garden for growing cabbage, beans, corn for roasting
ears, cucumbers, and potatoes. A log cabin, and, occasionally, a stable
and corn-crib, and a field of a dozen acres, the timber girdled or
"deadened," and fenced, are enough for his occupancy. It is quite
immaterial whether he ever becomes the owner of the soil. He is the
occupant for the time being, pays no rent, and feels as independent
as the "lord of the manor." With a horse, cow, and one or two breeders
of swine, he strikes into the woods with his family, and becomes the
founder of a new county, or perhaps state. He builds his cabin, gathers
around him a few other families of similar tastes and habits, and
occupies till the range is somewhat subdued, and hunting a little
precarious, or, which is more frequently the case, till the neighbors
crowd around, roads, bridges, and fields annoy him, and he lacks elbow
room. The preëmption law enables him to dispose of his cabin and
cornfield to the next class of emigrants; and, to employ his own figures,
he "breaks for the high timber," "clears out for the New Purchase,"

[34] Hale, "Daniel Boone" (pamphlet).

or migrates to Arkansas or Texas, to work the same process over.

The next class of emigrants purchase the lands, add field to field, clear out the roads, throw rough bridges over the streams, put up hewn log houses with glass windows and brick or stone chimneys, occasionally plant orchards, build mills, schoolhouses, court-houses, etc., and exhibit the picture and forms of plain, frugal, civilized life.

Another wave rolls on. The men of capital and enterprise come. The settler is ready to sell out and take the advantage of the rise in property, push farther into the interior and become, himself, a man of capital and enterprise in turn. The small village rises to a spacious town or city; substantial edifices of brick, extensive fields, orchards, gardens, colleges, and churches are seen. Broadcloths, silks, leghorns, crapes, and all the refinements, luxuries, elegancies, frivolities, and fashions are in vogue. Thus wave after wave is rolling westward; the real Eldorado is still farther on.

A portion of the two first classes remain stationary amidst the general movement, improve their habits and condition, and rise in the scale of society.

The writer has traveled much amongst the first class, the real pioneers. He has lived many years in connection with the second grade; and now the third wave is sweeping over large districts of Indiana, Illinois, and Missouri. Migration has become almost a habit in the West. Hundreds of men can be found, not over 50 years of age, who have settled for the fourth, fifth, or sixth time on a new spot. To sell out and remove only a few hundred miles makes up a portion of the variety of backwoods life and manners.[35]

Omitting those of the pioneer farmers who move from the love of adventure, the advance of the more steady farmer is easy to understand. Obviously the immigrant was attracted by the cheap lands of the frontier, and even the native farmer felt their influence strongly. Year by year the farmers who lived on soil whose returns were diminished by unrotated crops were offered the virgin soil of the frontier at nominal prices. Their growing families demanded more lands, and these were dear. The competition of the unexhausted, cheap, and easily tilled prairie lands compelled the farmer either to go west and continue the exhaustion of the soil on a new frontier, or to adopt intensive culture. Thus the census

[35] Compare Baily, "Tour in the Unsettled Parts of North America" (London, 1856), pp. 217–219, where a similar analysis is made for 1796. See also Collot, "Journey in North America" (Paris, 1826), p. 109; "Observations on the North American Land Company" (London, 1796), pp. xv, 144; Logan, "History of Upper South Carolina."

of 1890 shows in the Northwest many counties in which there is an absolute or a relative decrease of population. These States have been sending farmers to advance the frontier on the plains, and have themselves begun to turn to intensive farming and to manufacture. A decade before this, Ohio had shown the same transition stage. Thus the demand for land and the love of wilderness freedom drew the frontier ever onward.

Having now roughly outlined the various kinds of frontiers, and their modes of advance, chiefly from the point of view of the frontier itself, we may next inquire what were the influences on the East and on the Old World. A rapid enumeration of some of the more noteworthy effects is all that I have time for.

First, we note that the frontier promoted the formation of a composite nationality for the American people. The coast was preponderantly English, but the later tides of continental immigration flowed across to the free lands. This was the case from the early colonial days. The Scotch-Irish and the Palatine Germans, or "Pennsylvania Dutch," furnished the dominant element in the stock of the colonial frontier. With these peoples were also the freed indented servants, or redemptioners, who at the expiration of their time of service passed to the frontier. Governor Spottswood of Virginia writes in 1717, "The inhabitants of our frontiers are composed generally of such as have been transported hither as servants, and, being out of their time, settle themselves where land is to be taken up and that will produce the necessarys of life with little labour." [36] Very generally these redemptioners were of non-English stock. In the crucible of the frontier the immigrants were Americanized, liberated, and fused into a mixed race, English in neither nationality or characteristics. The process has gone on from the early days to our own. Burke and other writers in the middle of the eighteenth century believed that Pennsylvania[37] was "threatened with the danger of being wholly foreign in language, manners, and perhaps even inclinations." The German and Scotch-Irish elements in the frontier of the South were only less great. In the middle of the present century the German element in Wisconsin was already so considerable that leading publicists

[36] "Spottswood Papers," in Collections of Virginia Historical Society, i, ii.
[37] [Burke], "European Settlements" (1765 ed.), ii, p. 200.

looked to the creation of a German state out of the commonwealth by concentrating their colonization.[38] Such examples teach us to beware of misinterpreting the fact that there is a common English speech in America into a belief that the stock is also English.

In another way the advance of the frontier decreased our dependence on England. The coast, particularly of the South, lacked diversified industries and was dependent on England for the bulk of its supplies. In the South there was even a dependence on the Northern colonies for articles of food. Governor Glenn of South Carolina writes in the middle of the eighteenth century: "Our trade with New York and Philadelphia was of this sort, draining us of all the little money and bills we could gather from other places for their bread, flour, beer, hams, bacon, and other things of their produce, all which, except beer, our new townships begin to supply us with, which are settled with very industrious and thriving Germans. This no doubt diminishes the number of shipping and the appearance of our trade, but it is far from being a detriment to us." [39]

Before long the frontier created a demand for merchants. As it retreated from the coast it became less and less possible for England to bring her supplies directly to the consumer's wharfs and carry away staple crops, and staple crops began to give way to diversified agriculture for a time. The effect of this phase of the frontier action upon the northern section is perceived when we realize how the advance of the frontier aroused seaboard cities like Boston, New York, and Baltimore, to engage in rivalry for what Washington called "the extensive and valuable trade of a rising empire."

The legislation which most developed the powers of the National Government, and played the largest part in its activity, was conditioned on the frontier. Writers have discussed the subjects of tariff, land, and internal improvement, as subsidiary to the slavery question. But when American history comes to be rightly viewed it will be seen that the slavery question is an incident. In the period from the end of the first half of the present century to the close of the Civil War, slavery rose to primary, but far from

[38] Everest, in "Wisconsin Historical Collections," xii, pp. 7 ff.
[39] Weston, "Documents connected with History of South Carolina," p. 61.

exclusive, importance. But this does not justify Dr. von Holst (to take an example) in treating our constitutional history in its formative period down to 1828 in a single volume, giving six volumes chiefly to the history of slavery from 1828 to 1861, under the title "Constitutional History of the United States." The growth of nationalism and the evolution of American political institutions were dependent on the advance of the frontier. Even so recent a writer as Rhodes, in his "History of the United States since the Compromise of 1850," has treated the legislation called out by the western advance as incidental to the slavery struggle.

This is a wrong perspective. The pioneer needed the goods of the coast, and so the grand series of internal improvement and railroad legislation began, with potent nationalizing effects. Over internal improvements occurred great debates, in which grave constitutional questions were discussed. Sectional groupings appear in the votes, profoundly significant for the historian. Loose construction increased as the nation marched westward.[40] But the West was not content with bringing the farm to the factory. Under the lead of Clay—"Harry of the West"—protective tariffs were passed, with the cry of bringing the factory to the farm. The disposition of the public lands was a third important subject of national legislation influenced by the frontier.

The public domain has been a force of profound importance in the nationalization and development of the Government. The effects of the struggle of the landed and the landless states, and of the Ordinance of 1787, need no discussion.[41] Administratively the frontier called out some of the highest and most vitalizing activities of the General Government. The purchase of Louisiana was perhaps the constitutional turning point in the history of the Republic, inasmuch as it afforded both a new area for national legislation and the occasion of the downfall of the policy of strict construction. But the purchase of Louisiana was called out by frontier needs and demands. As frontier States accrued to the

[40] See, for example, the speech of Clay, in the House of Representatives, January 30, 1824.

[41] See the admirable monograph by Prof. H. B. Adams, "Maryland's Influence on the Land Cessions"; and also President Welling, in Papers American Historical Association, iii, p. 411.

Union, the national power grew. In a speech on the dedication of the Calhoun monument, Mr. Lamar explained: "In 1789 the States were the creators of the Federal Government; in 1861 the Federal Government was the creator of a large majority of the States."

When we consider the public domain from the point of view of the sale and disposal of the public lands, we are again brought face to face with the frontier. The policy of the United States in dealing with its lands is in sharp contrast with the European system of scientific administration. Efforts to make this domain a source of revenue, and to withhold it from emigrants in order that settlement might be compact, were in vain. The jealousy and the fears of the East were powerless in the face of the demands of the frontiersmen. John Quincy Adams was obliged to confess: "My own system of administration, which was to make the national domain the inexhaustible fund for progressive and unceasing internal improvement, has failed." The reason is obvious; a system of administration was not what the West demanded; it wanted land. Adams states the situation as follows: "The slaveholders of the South have bought the coöperation of the western country by the bribe of the western lands, abandoning to the new Western States their own proportion of the public property and aiding them in the design of grasping all the lands into their own hands. Thomas H. Benton was the author of this system, which he brought forward as a substitute for the American system of Mr. Clay, and to supplant him as the leading statesman of the West. Mr. Clay, by his tariff compromise with Mr. Calhoun, abandoned his own American system. At the same time he brought forward a plan for distributing among all the States of the Union the proceeds of the sales of the public lands. His bill for that purpose passed both Houses of Congress, but was vetoed by President Jackson, who, in his annual message of December, 1832, formally recommended that all public lands should be gratuitously given away to individual adventurers and to the States in which the lands are situated." [42]

"No subject," said Henry Clay, "which has presented itself to

[42] Adams Memoirs, ix, pp. 247, 248.

the present, or perhaps any preceding, Congress, is of greater magnitude than that of the public lands." When we consider the far-reaching effects of the Government's land policy upon political, economic, and social aspects of American life, we are disposed to agree with him. But this legislation was framed under frontier influences, and under the lead of Western statesmen like Benton and Jackson. Said Senator Scott of Indiana in 1841: "I consider the preëmption law merely declaratory of the custom or common law of the settlers."

It is safe to say that the legislation with regard to land, tariff, and internal improvements—the American system of the nationalizing Whig party—was conditioned on frontier ideas and needs. But it was not merely in legislative action that the frontier worked against the sectionalism of the coast. The economic and social characteristics of the frontier worked against sectionalism. The men of the frontier had closer resemblances to the Middle region than to either of the other sections. Pennsylvania had been the seed-plot of frontier emigration, and, although she passed on her settlers along the Great Valley into the west of Virginia and the Carolinas, yet the industrial society of these Southern frontiersmen was always more like that of the Middle region than like that of the tidewater portion of the South, which later came to spread its industrial type throughout the South.

The Middle region, entered by New York harbor, was an open door to all Europe. The tidewater part of the South represented typical Englishmen, modified by a warm climate and servile labor, and living in baronial fashion on great plantations; New England stood for a special English movement—Puritanism. The Middle region was less English than the other sections. It had a wide mixture of nationalities, a varied society, the mixed town and county system of local government, a varied economic life, many religious sects. In short, it was a region mediating between New England and the South, and the East and the West. It represented that composite nationality which the contemporary United States exhibits, that juxtaposition of non-English groups, occupying a valley or a little settlement, and presenting reflections of the map of Europe in their variety. It was democratic and nonsectional, if not national; "easy, tolerant, and contented"; rooted strongly in material prosperity. It was typical of the modern United States. It was least sectional, not only because it lay between North and South, but also because with no barriers to shut out its frontiers from its settled region, and with a system of connecting waterways, the Middle region mediated between East and West as well as between North and South. Thus it became the typically American region. Even the New Englander, who was shut out from the frontier by the Middle region, tarrying in New York or Pennsylvania on his westward march, lost the acuteness of his sectionalism on the way.[43]

The spread of cotton culture into the interior of the South finally broke down the contrast between the "tidewater" region and the rest of the State, and based Southern interests on slavery. Before this process revealed its results the western portion of the South, which was akin to Pennsylvania in stock, society, and industry, showed tendencies to fall away from the faith of the fathers into internal improvement legislation and nationalism. In the Virginia convention of 1829–30, called to revise the constitution, Mr. Leigh, of Chesterfield, one of the tidewater counties, declared:

One of the main causes of discontent which led to this convention, that which had the strongest influence in overcoming our veneration for the work of our fathers, which taught us to contemn the sentiments of Henry and Mason and Pendleton, which weaned us from our reverence for the constituted authorities of the State, was an overweening passion for internal improvement. I say this with perfect knowledge, for it has been avowed to me by gentlemen from the West over and over again. And let me tell the gentleman from Albemarle (Mr. Gordon) that it has been another principal object of those who set this ball of revolution in motion, to overturn the doctrine of State rights, of which Virginia has been the very pillar, and to remove the barrier she has interposed to the interference of the Federal Government in that same work of internal improvement, by so reorganizing the legislature that Virginia, too, may be hitched to the Federal car.

It was this nationalizing tendency of the West that transformed the democracy of Jefferson into the national republicanism of

[43] Author's article in *The Ægis* (Madison, Wis.), November 4, 1892.

Monroe and the democracy of Andrew Jackson. The West of the war of 1812, the West of Clay, and Benton, and Harrison, and Andrew Jackson, shut off by the Middle States and the mountains from the coast sections, had a solidarity of its own with national tendencies.[44] On the tide of the Father of Waters, North and South met and mingled into a nation. Interstate migration went steadily on—a process of cross-fertilization of ideas and institutions. The fierce struggle of the sections over slavery on the western frontier does not diminish the truth of this statement; it proves the truth of it. Slavery was a sectional trait that would not down, but in the West it could not remain sectional. It was the greatest of frontiersmen who declared: "I believe this Government can not endure permanently half slave and half free. It will become all of one thing or all of the other." Nothing works for nationalism like intercourse within the nation. Mobility of population is death to localism, and the western frontier worked irresistibly in unsettling population. The effect reached back from the frontier and affected profoundly the Atlantic coast and even the Old World.

But the most important effect of the frontier has been in the promotion of democracy here and in Europe. As has been indicated, the frontier is productive of individualism. Complex society is precipitated by the wilderness into a kind of primitive organization based on the family. The tendency is antisocial. It produces antipathy to control, and particularly to any direct control. The tax-gatherer is viewed as a representative of oppression. Prof. Osgood, in an able article,[45] has pointed out that the frontier conditions prevalent in the colonies are important factors in the explanation of the American Revolution, where individual liberty was sometimes confused with absence of all effective government. The same conditions aid in explaining the difficulty of instituting a strong government in the period of the confederacy. The frontier individualism has from the beginning promoted democracy.

The frontier States that came into the Union in the first quarter of a century of its existence came in with democratic suffrage

[44] Compare Roosevelt, "Thomas Benton," ch. i.
[45] *Political Science Quarterly,* ii, p. 457. Compare Sumner, "Alexander Hamilton," chs. ii-vii.

provisions, and had reactive effects of the highest importance upon the older States whose peoples were being attracted there. An extension of the franchise became essential. It was *western* New York that forced an extension of suffrage in the constitutional convention of that State in 1821; and it was *western* Virginia that compelled the tidewater region to put a more liberal suffrage provision in the constitution framed in 1830, and to give to the frontier region a more nearly proportionate representation with the tidewater aristocracy. The rise of democracy as an effective force in the nation came in with western preponderance under Jackson and William Henry Harrison, and it meant the triumph of the frontier—with all of its good and with all of its evil elements.[46] An interesting illustration of the tone of frontier democracy in 1830 comes from the same debates in the Virginia convention already referred to. A representative from western Virginia declared:

> But, sir, it is not the increase of population in the West which this gentleman ought to fear. It is the energy which the mountain breeze and western habits impart to those emigrants. They are regenerated, politically I mean, sir. They soon become *working politicians;* and the difference, sir, between a *talking* and a *working* politician is immense. The Old Dominion has long been celebrated for producing great orators; the ablest metaphysicians in policy; men that can split hairs in all abstruse questions of political economy. But at home, or when they return from Congress, they have negroes to fan them asleep. But a Pennsylvania, a New York, an Ohio, or a western Virginia statesman, though far inferior in logic, metaphysics, and rhetoric to an old Virginia statesman, has this advantage, that when he returns home he takes off his coat and takes hold of the plow. This gives him bone and muscle, sir, and preserves his republican principles pure and uncontaminated.

So long as free land exists, the opportunity for a competency exists, and economic power secures political power. But the democracy born of free land, strong in selfishness and individualism, intolerant of administrative experience and education, and pressing individual liberty beyond its proper bounds, has its dangers as well as its benefits. Individualism in America has allowed a laxity

[46] Compare Wilson, "Division and Reunion," pp. 15, 24.

in regard to governmental affairs which has rendered possible the spoils system and all the manifest evils that follow from the lack of a highly developed civic spirit. In this connection may be noted also the influence of frontier conditions in permitting lax business honor, inflated paper currency and wildcat banking. The colonial and revolutionary frontier was the region whence emanated many of the worst forms of an evil currency.[47] The West in the war of 1812 repeated the phenomenon on the frontier of that day, while the speculation and wildcat banking of the period of the crisis of 1837 occurred on the new frontier belt of the next tier of States. Thus each one of the periods of lax financial integrity coincides with periods when a new set of frontier communities had arisen, and coincides in area with these successive frontiers, for the most part. The recent Populist agitation is a case in point. Many a State that now declines any connection with the tenets of the Populists, itself adhered to such ideas in an earlier stage of the development of the State. A primitive society can hardly be expected to show the intelligent appreciation of the complexity of business interests in a developed society. The continual recurrence of these areas of paper-money agitation is another evidence that the frontier can be isolated and studied as a factor in American history of the highest importance.[48]

The East has always feared the result of an unregulated advance of the frontier, and has tried to check and guide it. The English authorities would have checked settlement at the headwaters of the Atlantic tributaries and allowed the "savages to enjoy their

[47] On the relation of frontier conditions to Revolutionary taxation, see Sumner, "Alexander Hamilton," ch. iii.

[48] I have refrained from dwelling on the lawless characteristics of the frontier, because they are sufficiently well known. The gambler and desperado, the regulators of the Carolinas and the vigilantes of California, are types of that line of scum that the waves of advancing civilization bore before them, and of the growth of spontaneous organs of authority where legal authority was absent. Compare Barrows, "United States of Yesterday and To-morrow"; Shinn, "Mining Camps"; and Bancroft, "Popular Tribunals." The humor, bravery, and rude strength, as well as the vices of the frontier in its worst aspect, have left traces on American character, language, and literature, not soon to be effaced.

deserts in quiet lest the peltry trade should decrease." This called out Burke's splendid protest:

If you stopped your grants, what would be the consequence? The people would occupy without grants. They have already so occupied in many places. You can not station garrisons in every part of these deserts. If you drive the people from one place, they will carry on their annual tillage and remove with their flocks and herds to another. Many of the people in the back settlements are already little attached to particular situations. Already they have topped the Appalachian Mountains. From thence they behold before them an immense plain, one vast, rich, level meadow; a square of five hundred miles. Over this they would wander without a possibility of restraint; they would change their manners with their habits of life; would soon forget a government by which they were disowned; would become hordes of English Tartars; and, pouring down upon your unfortified frontiers a fierce and irresistible cavalry, become masters of your governors and your counselers, your collectors and comptrollers, and of all the slaves that adhered to them. Such would, and in no long time must, be the effect of attempting to forbid as a crime and to suppress as an evil the command and blessing of Providence, "Increase and multiply." Such would be the happy result of an endeavor to keep as a lair of wild beasts that earth which God, by an express charter, has given to the children of men.

But the English Government was not alone in its desire to limit the advance of the frontier and guide its destinies. Tidewater Virginia[49] and South Carolina[50] gerrymandered those colonies to insure the dominance of the coast in their legislatures. Washington desired to settle a State at a time in the Northwest; Jefferson would reserve from settlement the territory of his Louisiana Purchase north of the thirty-second parallel, in order to offer it to the Indians in exchange for their settlements east of the Mississippi. "When we shall be full on this side," he writes, "we may lay off a range of States on the western bank from the head to the mouth, and so range after range, advancing compactly as we multiply." Madison went so far as to argue to the French minister that the United States had no interest in seeing population extend itself

[49] Debates in the Constitutional Convention, 1829-1830.
[50] [McCrady] Eminent and Representative Men of the Carolinas, i, p. 43; Calhoun's Works, i, pp. 401-406.

on the right bank of the Mississippi, but should rather fear it. When the Oregon question was under debate in 1824, Smyth, of Virginia, would draw an unchangeable line for the limits of the United States at the outer limit of two tiers of States beyond the Mississippi, complaining that the seaboard States were being drained of the flower of their population by the bringing of too much land into market. Even Thomas Benton, the man of widest views of the destiny of the West, at this stage of his career declared that along the ridge of the Rocky mountains "the western limits of the Republic should be drawn, and the statue of the fabled god Terminus should be raised upon its highest peak, never to be thrown down." [51] But the attempts to limit the boundaries, to restrict land sales and settlement, and to deprive the West of its share of political power were all in vain. Steadily the frontier of settlement advanced and carried with it individualism, democracy, and nationalism, and powerfully affected the East and the Old World.

The most effective efforts of the East to regulate the frontier came through its educational and religious activity, exerted by interstate migration and by organized societies. Speaking in 1835, Dr. Lyman Beecher declared: "It is equally plain that the religious and political destiny of our nation is to be decided in the West," and he pointed out that the population of the West "is assembled from all the States of the Union and from all the nations of Europe, and is rushing in like the waters of the flood, demanding for its moral preservation the immediate and universal action of those institutions which discipline the mind and arm the conscience and the heart. And so various are the opinions and habits, and so recent and imperfect is the acquaintance, and so sparse are the settlements of the West, that no homogeneous public sentiment can be formed to legislate immediately into being the requisite institutions. And yet they are all needed immediately in their utmost perfection and power. A nation is being 'born in a day.' . . . But what will become of the West if her prosperity rushes up to such a majesty of power, while those great institutions linger which are necessary to form the mind and the conscience and the

[51] Speech in the Senate, March 1, 1825; Register of Debates, i, 721.

heart of that vast world. It must not be permitted. . . . Let no man at the East quiet himself and dream of liberty, whatever may become of the West. . . . Her destiny is our destiny." [52]

With the appeal to the conscience of New England, he adds appeals to her fears lest other religious sects anticipate her own. The New England preacher and schoolteacher left their mark on the West. The dread of Western emancipation from New England's political and economic control was paralleled by her fears lest the West cut loose from her religion. Commenting in 1850 on reports that settlement was rapidly extending northward in Wisconsin, the editor of the *Home Missionary* writes: "We scarcely know whether to rejoice or mourn over this extension of our settlements. While we sympathize in whatever tends to increase the physical resources and prosperity of our country, we can not forget that with all these dispersions into remote and still remoter corners of the land the supply of the means of grace is becoming relatively less and less." Acting in accordance with such ideas, home missions were established and Western colleges were erected. As seaboard cities like Philadelphia, New York, and Baltimore strove for the mastery of Western trade, so the various denominations strove for the possession of the West. Thus an intellectual stream from New England sources fertilized the West. Other sections sent their missionaries; but the real struggle was between sects. The contest for power and the expansive tendency furnished to the various sects by the existence of a moving frontier must have had important results on the character of religious organization in the United States. The multiplication of rival churches in the little frontier towns had deep and lasting social effects. The religious aspects of the frontier make a chapter in our history which needs study.

From the conditions of frontier life came intellectual traits of profound importance. The works of travelers along each frontier from colonial days onward describe certain common traits, and these traits have, while softening down, still persisted as survivals in the place of their origin, even when a higher social organization

[52] Plea for the West (Cincinnati, 1835), pp. 11 ff.

succeeded. The result is that to the frontier the American intellect owes its striking characteristics. That coarseness and strength combined with acuteness and inquisitiveness; that practical, inventive turn of mind, quick to find expedients; that masterful grasp of material things, lacking in the artistic but powerful to effect great ends; that restless, nervous energy;[53] that dominant individualism, working for good and for evil, and withal that buoyancy and exuberance which comes with freedom—these are traits of the frontier, or traits called out elsewhere because of the existence of the frontier. Since the days when the fleet of Columbus sailed into the waters of the New World, America has been another name for opportunity, and the people of the United States have taken their tone from the incessant expansion which has not only been open but has even been forced upon them. He would be a rash prophet who should assert that the expansive character of American life has now entirely ceased. Movement has been its dominant fact, and, unless this training has no effect upon a people, the American energy will continually demand a wider field for its exercise. But never again will such gifts of free land offer themselves. For a moment, at the frontier, the bonds of custom are broken and unrestraint is triumphant. There is not *tabula rasa*. The stubborn American environment is there with its imperious summons to accept its conditions; the inherited ways of doing things are also there; and yet, in spite of environment, and in spite of custom, each frontier did indeed furnish a new field of opportunity, a gate of escape from the bondage of the past; and freshness, and confidence, and scorn of older society, impatience of its restraints and its ideas, and indifference to its lessons, have accompanied the frontier. What the Mediterranean Sea was to the Greeks, breaking

[53] Colonial travelers agree in remarking on the phlegmatic characteristics of the colonists. It has frequently been asked how such a people could have developed that strained nervous energy now characteristic of them. Compare Sumner, "Alexander Hamilton," p. 98, and Adams, "History of the United States," i, p. 60; ix, pp. 240, 241. The transition appears to become marked at the close of the War of 1812, a period when interest centered upon the development of the West, and the West was noted for restless energy. Grund, "Americans," ii, ch. i.

the bond of custom, offering new experiences, calling out new institutions and activities, that, and more, the ever retreating frontier has been to the United States directly, and to the nations of Europe more remotely. And now, four centuries from the discovery of America, at the end of a hundred years of life under the Constitution, the frontier has gone, and with its going has closed the first period of American history.

Personal Competition

CHARLES HORTON COOLEY

Charles Horton Cooley (1864–1929) was the son of an eminent jurist, Thomas M. Cooley, member of the supreme court of Michigan, a leading authority on constitutional law, and first chairman of the Interstate Commerce Commission. Cooley himself was born in Ann Arbor and received all his university training there at the state university, where he taught sociology throughout his academic career. To many he seemed remote and detached from the life around him, but with him, as with Veblen, what seemed detachment was often a knife to slash into his own time to the quick; a colleague recalled of Cooley: "I once heard him in a lecture liken the modern pursuit of wealth to the Children's Crusade of the Middle Ages." The selections here are Parts I, II, III, and IX of a monograph published in American Economic Association, *Economic Studies,* IV, No. 2 (New York, 1899).

THE FUNCTION OF PERSONAL COMPETITION

THE FUNCTION of personal competition, considered as a part of the social system, is to assign to each individual his place in that system. If "all the world's a stage," this is a process that distributes the parts among the players. It may do it well or ill, but, after some fashion, it does it. Some may be cast in parts unsuited to them; good actors may be discharged altogether and worse ones retained; but nevertheless the thing is arranged in some way and the play goes on.

That such a process must exist can hardly, it seems to me, admit of question: in fact I believe that those who speak of doing away with competition use the word in another sense than is here intended. Within the course of the longest human life there is necessarily a complete renewal of the persons whose communication and cooperation make up the life of society. The new members come into the world without any legible sign to indicate what they are fit for, a mystery to others from the first and to themselves as soon as they are capable of reflection: the young man does not know for what he is adapted, and no one else can tell him. The only possible way to get light upon the matter is to adopt the method of experiment. By trying one thing and another and by reflecting upon his experience, he begins to find out about himself, and the world begins to find out about him. His field of investigation is of course restricted, and his own judgment and that of others liable to error, but the tendency of it all can hardly be other than to guide his choice to that one of the available careers in which he is best adapted to hold his own. I may say this much, perhaps, without assuming anything regarding the efficiency or justice of competition as a distributor of social functions, a matter regarding which I shall offer some suggestions later. All I wish to say here is that the necessity of some selective process is inherent in the conditions of social life.

It will be apparent that, in the sense in which I use the term, competition is not necessarily a hostile contention, nor even something of which the competing individual is always conscious. From our infancy onward throughout life, judgments are daily forming regarding us of which we are unaware, but which go to determine our careers. "The world is full of judgment days." A and B, for instance, are under consideration for some appointment: the experience and personal qualifications of each are duly weighed by those having the appointment to make, and A, we will say, is chosen. Neither of the two need know anything about the matter until the selection is made. It is eligibility to perform some social function that makes a man a competitor, and he may or may not be aware of it, or, if aware of it, he may or may not be consciously opposed to others. I trust that the reader will bear in mind that I always use the word *competition* in the sense here explained.

There is but one alternative to competition as a means of determining the place of the individual in the social system, and that is some form of *status,* some fixed, mechanical rule, usually a rule of inheritance, which decides the function of the individual without reference to his personal traits, and thus dispenses with any process of comparison.[1] It is possible to conceive of a society[2] organized entirely upon the basis of the inheritance of functions, and indeed societies exist which may be said to approach this condition. In India, for example, the prevalent idea regarding the social function of the individual is that it is unalterably determined by his parentage, and the village blacksmith, shoemaker, accountant or priest has his place assigned to him by a rule of descent as rigid as that which governs the transmission of one of the crowns of Europe. If all functions were handed down in this way, if there were never any deficiency or surplus of children to take the place of their parents, if there were no progress or decay in the social system, making necessary new activities or dispensing with old ones; then, there would be no use for a selective process. But precisely in the measure that a society departs from this condition, that individual traits are recognized and made available, or social change of any sort comes to pass, in that measure must there be competition.

Status is not an active process as competition is; it is simply a rule of conservation, a makeshift to avoid the inconveniences of continual readjustment in the social structure. Competition or selection is the only constructive principle, and everything worthy the name of organization had at some time or other a competitive origin. At the present day the eldest son of a peer may succeed to a seat in the House of Lords simply by right of birth; but his ancestor got the seat by competition, by some exercise of personal

[1] The principle of length of service, so widely recognized in making promotions, is an example of a form of *status* unconnected with inheritance.

[2] As there has been much discussion concerning the meaning of this word it may be well to say that I use it, with conscious vagueness, to mean a totality of social relations. I also use the terms "social order" and "social system" in the same sense.

qualities that made him valued, or loved, or feared, by a king
or a minister.

Sir Henry Maine has pointed out that the increase of competition is a characteristic trait of modern life, and that the powerful
ancient societies of the old world were for the most part non-
competitive in their structure. While this is true, it would be a
mistake to draw the inference that *status* is a peculiarly natural
or primitive principle of organization and competition a comparatively recent discovery. On the contrary the spontaneous
relations among men, as we see in the case of children, and as
we may infer from the life of the lower animals, are highly competitive, personal prowess and ascendency being everything and little
regard being paid to descent simply as such. The *régime* of
inherited *status,* on the other hand, is a comparatively complex
and artificial product, necessarily of later growth, whose very
general prevalence among the successful societies of the old world
is doubtless to be explained by the stability and consequently the
power which it was calculated to give to the social system. It
survived because under certain conditions it was the fittest. It was
not and is not universally predominant among savage or barbarous
peoples. With the American Indians, for example, the definiteness
and authority of *status* were comparatively small, personal prowess
and initiative being correspondingly important. The interesting
monograph on Omaha Sociology by Dorsey, published by the
United States Bureau of Ethnology, contains many facts showing
that the life of this people was highly competitive. When the tribe
was at war any brave could organize an expedition against the
enemy, if he could induce enough others to join him, and this
organizer usually assumed the command. In a similar way the
managers of the hunt were chosen because of personal skill; and
in general "Any man can win a name and rank in the state by
becoming 'wacuce' or brave, either in war or by the bestowal of
gifts and the frequent giving of feasts."

Throughout history there has been a struggle between the
principles of *status* and competition regarding the part that each
should play in the social system. Generally speaking the advantage
of *status* is in its power to give order and continuity. As Gibbon
informs us, "The superior prerogative of birth, when it has ob-

tained the sanction of time and popular opinion, is the plainest and least invidious of all distinctions among mankind";[3] and he is doubtless right in ascribing the confusion of the later Roman Empire largely to the lack of an established rule for the transmission of imperial authority. The chief danger of *status* is that of suppressing personal development, and so of causing social enfeeblement, rigidity and ultimate decay. On the other hand, competition develops the individual and gives flexibility and animation to the social order; its danger being chiefly that of disintegration in some form or other. The general tendency in modern times has been toward the relative increase of the free or competitive principle, owing to the fact that the rise of other means of securing stability has diminished the need for *status*. The latter persists, however, even in the freest countries, as the method by which wealth is transmitted, and also in social classes, which, so far as they exist at all, are based chiefly upon inherited wealth and the culture and opportunities that go with it. The ultimate reason for this persistence—without very serious opposition—in the face of the obvious inequalities and limitations upon liberty that it perpetuates, is perhaps the fact that no other method of transmission has arisen that has shown itself capable of giving continuity and order to the control of wealth.

THE INTENSITY OF COMPETITION

By the intensity of competition I mean the relative amount of activity absorbed by the selective process. To make this meaning clearer suppose a country where children ordinarily remain in the same locality as their parents, where their choice of career is practically limited to a small number of trades or, in the case of the upper class, to three or four professions; where, moreover, one who has established himself in a trade or profession is fairly secure against being driven out of it, or of finding it undermined by new methods; there, I should say, the intensity of competition is small, that is to say each man devotes but a small part of his energy to finding his place in the social whole. That question is in great measure settled for him by the conditions just mentioned.

[3] *Decline and Fall,* Milman-Smith Edition, i, 305.

On the other hand, if neither place nor class confine him, if migration in search of opportunity is common, if the humblest-born may and do aspire to the highest places, and spend a large part of their lives in striving to attain them, if a man even when established in some niche in the social system can maintain it only by vigorous and continued endeavor; there the intensity of competition is great. Again, where things go on in much the same way one generation after another, without the creation of new kinds of activity or the extension of old ones, competition will be less intense than where a rapid creation of new functions involves selection to determine who shall perform them.

The greater or less efficiency of the selective agents is another important element in the matter. If they work promptly and surely, they may do a great deal with a comparatively small expenditure of force, and the intensity of competition will be correspondingly diminished; while if they are inefficient, they will, like any other bad machine, use up a great deal of energy without producing a corresponding result.

Accordingly it seems to me that the general relation between social conditions and the intensity of competition may be comprised in the following propositions:

The intensity of competition varies

1. with the degree of personal liberty;
2. with the rate of social change;
3. inversely as the efficiency of the selective agents.

The freer the individual the wider his field of choice in determining his social function, and the wider the field of choice the more active must the selective process be in assigning him his place in it. Of a child born in British India, it can be predicted with some probability what and where he will be thirty years hence; but a child born in an American village may be anywhere and anything, almost, at the end of that time: no one would venture a guess. In the one case competition has little to do; in the other everything. So with social change; unless it is mere decay, it involves new things to be done, new opportunities. For example, the electric industries, now employing hundreds of thousands of men, have arisen within a comparatively short time, and every man in them has found his place by competition. In an analogous manner the opening of new regions, like Oklahoma or the Klondike, the creation of an army, such as took place at the outbreak of the Spanish war, the revelation of new fields of research, such as was made by the publication of the *Origin of Species,* are inevitably the occasion of a selective activity to determine who shall be the settlers, the miners, the military officers, the investigators, that the situation demands.[4]

As to selective agencies, an all-wise despot would undoubtedly be the most efficient; and it is conceivable that he might give to men a great deal of personal liberty and provide for any amount of social change without much increase in the intensity of competition. This being out of the question, a society striving to be free and progressive must do the best it can to achieve rational selections through its organization. By just laws, by a public sentiment appreciative of every sort of merit, and, most of all, by a system of education calculated to discover and develop the special capabilities of each individual, it can do much to make its choices prompt, intelligent and just, and to avoid wasteful conflict. It is from this point of view that the existing state of things has been most effectively criticised; and writers who demand that competition be suppressed usually mean that we ought to replace irrational and destructive contention by intelligent selection.

The three propositions that I have suggested indicate the social conditions of more-or-less intensified competition. To these should be added a condition that is rather biological or psychological, namely the race traits of the people. An aggressive, ambitious, virile people, such as the Anglo-Saxon, German or Irish, is naturally competitive. Each man wants a great deal, and has little dread of migration, hardship, uncertainty, or personal contention, to deter him from seeking it. An Englishman or a German will seize upon all the opportunities in sight and demand more, where an Italian or a Spaniard would perhaps make no use of those that are at hand.

---

[4] A local and temporary intensification of competition may result from a diminution of opportunity which forces many individuals to struggle for access to a few openings. This is perhaps what some people would be likely to think of in connection with the phrase "intense competition." But the changes which give a general and enduring stimulus to competition are of the opposite sort, are such as increase opportunity.

The principles above stated are sufficient to explain the fact, which seems to me unquestionable, that the present time is one when, among all progressive peoples, competition is far more intense than it has ever been in the past. They also explain why it is much more intense in some countries than in others, and in some parts of those countries than in other parts.

The diffusion of personal freedom among the mass of the people is undoubtedly, it seems to me, something that was never achieved on any large scale or for any long period until within the present century. Such democracies as existed previously were small, of short duration, and at best gave comparatively little real personal liberty. The fundamental reason for this general failure of free institutions in the past I believe to be the fact that until modern methods of easy and rapid communication came into existence it was impossible to combine freedom with unity, order and control over wide areas. The unfree individual is controlled by custom, authority, physical necessity and other agencies that do not involve his intelligent choice: the free individual must be controlled by what we call the moral forces, by public opinion, patriotism, rational self-interest and the like. Now nothing but the newspaper, the telegraph, the railroad and the rest of the modern appliance of communication can enable the moral forces to be so organized as to act quickly and effectively over wide areas. Consequently freedom on a great scale was an impossibility in the past, and the large, stable, powerful states were based on *status* and authority. Personal freedom failed because it was the unfit; it is now succeeding because, under changed conditions, it has become the fit.

This is hardly the place to develop this view of the genesis of personal liberty, though I feel confident that it will recommend itself to the reflective reader. In the meantime it is certain that such liberty has increased rapidly and that it has correspondingly stimulated competition. Of the great nations the United States has undoubtedly partaken most fully of this tendency, Great Britain next, and Germany perhaps next. It is now well understood that the Latin nations, even republican France, are behind the Teutonic nations in this respect; the chief cause apparently being something in the race psychology of the two stocks. We find that in France, notwithstanding her unstable politics, the social life as a whole is quieter, based more on status and less on competition, than in the other countries mentioned. France "presents the spectacle of a tranquil people with agitated legislators." [5]

The first principle, then, gives one reason for intense competitive activity in the United States: a consideration of the second will show how greatly this activity is stimulated by social change. The changes that this country is undergoing may be divided into two classes: those that are world-wide, which it shares with other countries that are in the current; and local changes incident to the development of a new country. The former have intensified competition everywhere; the latter give it a peculiar vigor and a special character among us.

The thought of the industrial revolution and of the radical social changes of every sort that have grown out of it is so familiar that I do not care to dwell upon it. Not industry only but family life, social relations, science, education, philosophy and religion are in process of transformation as a result of this movement. In all these fields, though most consciously in industry—because that gives occupation to the vast majority of the people—we have intenser activity, more striving, more success and more failure, a constant breaking-up of settled relations. Great cities, which are incidental products of the new *régime,* are in all countries the *foci* of competition, and show most conspicuously its good and evil results. Populated by immigrants, tradition and *status* have little hold upon them, either for good or evil: their industries, their institutions, their social and moral conditions, are new and un-regulated.

To all this a new country adds the special series of changes incident to the passage of each part of it through those steps of development, from the rude agriculture of pioneers to the full maturity of manufacturers and commerce, which would suffice to produce a restless and competitive condition of things, even if the course of life in older countries were quite uniform and regular. This series is so mingled with the other that it cannot well be studied separately, but its influence appears clearly in the general result. It is chiefly, I think, because they have this additional strain upon them that Americans are thinner, quicker, more

[5] Quoted in Bodley's *France,* i, 57.

nervous and restless than their English kinsmen; it is for this reason, I should say, rather than on account of the difference in climate, that people walk faster upon the streets of Chicago than upon the streets of London; and this helps to explain, also, why, in spite of an unequalled expenditure of ability and energy, so much remains undone in the United States that other nations have achieved.

And moreover the disintegration that accompanies all these changes affects the selective process itself, and tends in some measure to exaggerate the intensity of competition and lower its character by making it wasteful, unjust, brutal, anarchical. The just laws, the effective moral sentiment adapted to the various conditions of human activity, the adequate educational institutions, which ought to preside over and assist competition, being things of slow growth, are largely wanting just when they are most needed; and we have as a result the disorganization which is so often portrayed, not without some extravagance, by the advocates of radical reconstruction.

Whether this great intensity of competition is on the whole a good or a bad thing cannot be determined satisfactorily until the period is past and we can see what comes of it; perhaps not then. The matter will frequently come up in the further course of this essay. In general it may be said here that the present *régime* certainly does great things for those individuals whom nature and training have fitted to thrive in it, developing energy, self-reliance, strength of character and power and efficiency of many sorts; but bears with blind severity upon the weak, the misplaced and the unprepared, among whom are many who in circumstances more fortunate would take an honorable and important part in the general life. The moral and social forces that should prepare and support men share in the general disturbance and disintegration; character as well as ability is mercilessly and unfairly tried, and the access of strength to those that stand the test is more or less offset by the demoralization and degeneration of those who do not. Whole classes of the population, institutions, nations, modes of thought, may suffer retrogression. Thus it may not be true, as some believe, that the Negro race has deteriorated under the moral strain of emancipation, but there is nothing absurd in the hypothesis. Or we may plausibly ascribe the pessimism and sensualism of French literature to a decay of religious faith which has not been made good by the adequate growth of other elevating influences. Local retrogression undoubtedly exists all about us. There is strong evidence that certain portions of our immigrant population suffer moral deterioration, perhaps temporary, under the influence of American life. Corrupt conditions of business are common enough, though not so general as many suppose, and are found principally in new industries, new forms of association and, in general, where business morality has not had sufficient opportunity to develop. Political corruption, which flourishes most in great cities and among immigrant populations, may be looked upon as coming in part under the same general law. To discuss these questions fully would take us too far; it will be easily understood that a thorough examination of the effects of intense competition would bring within our range all the pressing social problems of our time.

Meanwhile it is well not to forget that even in the United States this restless activity is by no means general, but is confined to the frontiers of social change. The majority of the people live in rural communities and, though more wide awake and changeful than rural populations elsewhere, are not in danger of demoralization by excessive mental strain. While very intense competition is a characteristic of the time and place—that is, there is more of it here and now than elsewhere or ever before—it is far from being universal.

We must also bear in mind in this connection that any diminution of the intensity of competition is inevitably accompanied by an advance in the alternative principle of *status*. In our eastern states, as conditions become more settled, social classes are correspondingly delimited. The family line, always the most tenacious strand in the social fabric, renews its continuity and its hold upon tradition, fellow-feeling, and other parts of the social structure; inherited wealth and position create differences in education, manners and associations; and the resulting class sentiment prevents free intermarriage and increases the difficulty of rising from the manual laboring to the professional and commercial class.[6]

I do not mean to imply that we have here merely a see-saw

[6] See A. F. Sanborn, "A Massachusetts Shoe Town," *Atlantic Monthly,* August, 1897.

between alternative evils. It is possible to combine, in a considerable degree, the advantages of competition with those of stability, to keep opportunity open after tranquillity is assured. For example, a system of free technical education which should bring home to every boy in the land the opportunity to secure the best training in any career for which his natural capacity fits him, would promote competition of the best kind without producing any serious ill to offset the good. The question of good or ill is quite a different one from the question of *status* or competition: either of these principles may work very well or very badly. We must try to combine the better forms of each in such a way as to produce the best general result.

Nevertheless it would certainly indicate a lack of insight if a person who deprecated intense competition of all kinds as a great evil should also attack such strongholds of *status* as the inheritance of property and class sentiment; since any demolition of these portions of the social structure must inevitably be compensated by increased competition of some kind or other. There are no other organizing principles in society beside these, and what one does not do the other must. If wealth, for example, were not inherited, the death of a rich man would call for some sort of a selective process to determine what person or persons should control his estate; just as the substitution of a president chosen by the people for a hereditary monarch involves increased competition in the form of elections.

THE RELATION OF COMPETITION TO ASSOCIATION

Where there is a common interest, it is rational to pursue it through united action. There is at present no necessity to combat the error, ascribed to the classical school of English economists, that competition is the natural state of man and combination something irregular and unnatural. The tendency is perhaps rather toward the opposite error, namely, that of assuming that competition is the irregular and unnatural thing and combination alone normal. The two, of course, are supplementary and each has its proper sphere. One is achievement, the other process. Competition is an organizing force, and its relation to association is—as Hamerton said of the relation of truth to beauty in art—one of inferior rank but prior necessity.

The usual way of thinking and writing about these two appears to flow from an idea of separateness and inconsistency between them that does not correspond with the facts. Though perfectly distinct as principles, they are inextricably interlaced in human life. Every one of us is a competitor in several or many fields, while he is at the same time a member of various co-operating groups: and—what seems somewhat surprising—we are likely to compete with the very persons with whom we co-operate. For example, every important branch of trade has a rather elaborate system of co-operation, including associations, trade journals, price agreements, and the like; yet it is among those who follow the same trade that competition is most severe. Again, here is a factory full of operatives joined together in a labor union for the furtherance of common interests; yet they inevitably compete among themselves—for reputation as workmen and advancement in grade, for office or influence in the union, and probably in many ways not directly connected with their work. It is the same with any active group. The faculty of a university is an illustration of organized co-operation of the highest type; but there is always competition among its members, for the furtherance of individual views of educational policy, for professional reputation, and the like. As I have pointed out, no active person escapes competition for a day. It goes on often when he is quite unconscious of it: that is, his action is affecting judgments and influences that will ultimately determine, in some measure, his social function and career.

Nor is there anything irrational in this interlacing of the two principles. It is rational to co-operate as regards common interests, and at the same time to compete as regards interests which are divergent or undetermined; and this is what men do.

Co-operation, then, arises when men see that they have a common interest, and have at the same time sufficient intelligence and self-control to seek this interest through united action: perceived unity of interest and the faculty of organization are the essential factors in intelligent combination. This power of timely and effective "getting together" is one of the things that chiefly distinguish the abler races of men from the weaker, and would of itself suffice as a test by which to arrange the various nations of the earth in an ascending scale of ability. With good reason, we congratulate ourselves that the American people, as a result both of nature and training, possess this faculty in a comparatively high degree, although they are at the same time a notably competitive people. There is nothing inconsistent in this: to compete vigorously and combine promptly is to be expected of men who are at once aggressive, sympathetic and intelligent.

Because it requires intelligence and energy, because it is difficult, intelligent co-operation always lags behind the need for it; and we have the rule that competition, once set up, is likely to persist beyond the point where it ought to be dispensed with.[7] Owing to this fact it is, in our own time, not only intense but quite often excessive: it continues when it might better yield to co-operation. When the selective process has performed its function, when it has answered the question, what is the fittest, as well as it can, it ought to cease and give place to organization. To prolong it beyond this point is wasteful and destructive, the principle involved being the same as that rule of humane warfare which declares that the sacrifice of life ought not to continue when the result ceases to be doubtful. The failure to cease is an evil characteristic of a time like the present when the work of breaking down obstructive organization, the outworn machinery of the past, has been pretty well accomplished, and the time for reorganization has arrived. During the breaking-down period the great need is to introduce the competitive principle; but when this has been achieved, and the building-up period has set in, the great need is to check it. If we look about us we see almost everywhere a condition of disintegration, of working at cross purposes, which gives much color to the views of those who charge the age with "anarchical individualism" and call for repressive control. Trades unions, for instance, are far from performing their proper functions: the lower grades of labor being unorganized, and the unions among the higher frequently unstable and apparently ill-conducted. In almost

[7] In this connection the reader will recall the notable essay by Professor Giddings on "The Persistence of Competition," in the *Political Science Quarterly* for March, 1887.

every branch of trade competing agencies are multiplied beyond what is necessary or economical: there seem to be too many small groceries, drug stores, hardware stores, shoe stores, restaurants and the like; that is, the goods they supply could be furnished cheaper if the same energy were concentrated upon fewer establishments. It is well known that more railroads have been built, in many instances, than there is any need for; and the rate-wars that frequently take place have been shown to be injurious to the public as well as to the stockholders. We hear also that there are too many small churches, too many small colleges; and so on.

This state of things is slowly working its own remedy: the tendency, the current, is clearly toward organization. This is decidedly a time of "getting together," though the results so far achieved are small compared with what is needed. It is surprising to note the number and variety of conventions that take place in one of our larger cities during the summer months. From the advancement of science to billposting, almost every reputable occupation seems to have general interests which require the attendance of delegates at an annual meeting; not to speak of the hundreds of social and benevolent societies. The rise of department stores, the multiplication of private industrial corporations and the formation of trusts are, of course, an outcome of the same tendency. Organization, since it brings power and success, is coming rapidly; and the very process of its coming introduces a new set of problems, *problems of symmetry in growth.* Some forms of organization, like the private corporations just mentioned, outstrip other forms which are required to balance or control them—legislation, for instance, administrative machinery, economic science, trades-unions—and we have an overweening growth of power, which gives rise to much wrong, much protest and to extravagant projects of reform. In this lack of symmetry, this narrowing of contemporary development into a few channels while others are almost dried up, is to be found the cause of many if not most of the evils characteristic of our time.

I am as far from sharing the apprehensions of those who see a "coming slavery" in the growth of organization as I am from joining in the indiscriminate condemnation of competition. No fear need be entertained of the disappearance of competition:

it is quite as firmly rooted as association. The two will continue to subsist side by side while varying indefinitely in form and character. Those who cry "Look out for slavery!" as well as those who cry "Look out for anarchy!" are seeing ghosts which will hardly materialize. The future will have its urgent problems, of which the problem of the regulation of great associations will certainly be one, but there is no reason to despair of accomplishing this regulation, and much reason to hope that, if properly regulated, the development of rational organization will increase and not diminish the freedom of the individual.

The proposition that competition is an organizing force or process appears, at first sight, to be opposed to the views of some very distinguished writers from whom I should be sorry to find myself at variance; but I think this apparent opposition is more a matter of difference in the use of terms than anything else. The word *competition* is used by them as equivalent to what I should call bad competition; and their projects of dispensing with competition are such as I should describe as projects for displacing a lower form by a higher. Professor Lester F. Ward, by a very striking comparison, has vividly illustrated the principle that the mere blind struggle for existence, the natural selection of the animal or vegetable worlds, is suited only to the early stages of organic progress, and becomes wasteful and repressive when continued beyond the point where it can be replaced by intelligent selection. He says:

Once, when herborizing in a rather wild, neglected spot, I collected a little depauperate grass that for a time greatly puzzled me, but which upon analysis proved to be none other than genuine wheat. It had been accidentally sown in this abandoned nook, where it had been obliged to struggle for existence along with the remaining vegetation. There it had grown up and sought to rise into that majesty and beauty that is seen in a field of waving grain. But at every step it had felt the resistance of an environment no longer regulated by intelligence. It missed the fostering care of man, who destroys competition, removes enemies, and creates conditions favorable to the highest development. This is called cultivation, and the difference between my little starveling grass and the wheat of the well-tilled field, is a difference of cultivation only, and not at all of capacity. . . . I look upon existing humanity as I look upon a pristine vegetation. The whole struggling mass is held by the relentless laws of competition in a condition far below its possibilities. Just as what might be grain is mere grass, just as the potential greening is a diminutive crab-apple, so the potential giants of the intellectual world may now be the hewers of wood and the drawers of water.[8]

The remedy Professor Ward shows to be education, in the broadest and truest sense of the word, the surrounding of each individual with that environment most favorable to the development of his faculties.

I sympathize heartily with the views thus eloquently set forth.[9] If the selective process is to be progressive and not retrograde in its tendency it must pass continually to higher and higher levels as society advances; it must become more rational, more economical, more moral, more just, more free. In the present connection, however, it is fair to add—what I imagine Professor Ward would readily admit—that in point of difficulty, social selection presents a wide contrast with the case of the wheat, and that existing competition, bad as it is in many respects, has a relative justification, or at least an explanation, in the fact that it is the only organizing agency available. Some of the points of contrast that I have in mind are the following:

1. Social selection must have in view not one simple type of excellence to be preserved and developed, but an enormous number of divergent types, matching the complexity of social functions. Not the wheat only, but every species and variety of plant that grows calls for a garden plot of its own, and a special culture. We scarcely dare assert that there are any weeds at all on the social roadside, some authors holding that every child that is born is fitted to take some useful part in the general life. We can transplant and arrange, trying to accommodate each so far as practicable in the matter of soil and climate, but selection, as the wheat is selected, involves the suppression of other species, and that, in view of the complexity of which I speak, we scarcely dare attempt. If the problem were to develop large men, or strong men, or blue-eyed

[8] "Broadening the Way to Success," *The Forum,* December, 1886.
[9] I have maintained views somewhat similar, as regards fundamental conceptions, in an essay on "Genius, Fame and the Comparison of Races," published in the *Annals of the American Academy of Political and Social Science,* May, 1897.

men, or mathematicians, or musicians, and we could rank all
other types as weeds and mercilessly plow them up, the matter
would be quite simple and easy. But because such arbitrary selection of types to be favored would be intolerable, we put up with
a somewhat blind and anarchical struggle as the lesser evil. In
short, we cannot select rationally because we do not know what
we want. We know very well what we wish to get out of a grain
of wheat, but in the case of a child we do not know.

2. In the case of man there are no visible external traits or
"characters" which can be used as trustworthy guides to selection.
Darwin, in *The Origin of Species,* noted the reliance upon such
traits as a weakness of all artificial selection; and in the social order
this weakness becomes so pronounced as to be absolutely fatal to
all schemes for setting an *a priori* valuation upon men. The most
plausible principle of *a priori* valuation, that of heredity, which
was so generally adopted in the past, is of course hopelessly
discredited as a basis for social organization. Because of this lack
of reliable signs to go by, social selection can never be the simple
act of a presiding intelligence, like the selection by man of types of
animals or plants but must be competitive, in so far as that each
person must be permitted and assisted to form his own idea of
what he is fit for, and to show what he can do by doing it. We
want a competition that shall bring a gentle but firm pressure to
bear upon all persons, urging *and aiding* them to find something
useful that they are fit to do, and then to do it faithfully.
Progress, as Professor Ward so warmly urges, must be along the
line of a scientific educational process which shall not so much
select for the individual as help him to select for himself; and the
test, to find out by comparison with others whether he has chosen
rightly or not, can never, it seems to me, be dispensed with.

3. It is scarcely necessary, perhaps, to add that even if the
problem were soluble from a scientific standpoint, the practical
treatment of if would remain extremely difficult on account of
the lack of a single, paramount and intelligent will to play the
part of the wise despot who plants the wheat and ploughs up the
other grasses. The "sociocracy" which Professor Ward has taught
us to look to as the instrument of rational progress must clearly be

somewhat slow in its growth, the ripe achievement of an intelligent, self-controlled and well-organized democracy. In the meantime we must do the best we can.

Another point which ought to be considered in estimating the work which competition, as an organizing process, has to do, is the degree of natural adaptation that may be assumed to exist between the innate capacities of men and the society in which these capacities are to play a part. The optimistic view is that there is a place for everyone, and that the only question is how to get everyone in his place; that each man has some special aptitude that only needs opportunity for development to make him both happy and useful. Thus as each one has properly a distinct object of ambition different from that of everyone else, "every man, by his success in the pursuit, does not hinder but helps his competitors." "Every individual has a bias which he must obey, and it is only as he feels and obeys this that he rightly develops and attains his legitimate power in the world." [10] The competitive process is thus conceived in its highest form, as an amicable testing and comparison of powers, with a view to securing the happiness of all by helping each to find his own peculiar and appropriate work. It is like the preliminary practice of a football team to determine what place shall be assigned to each player: everyone, presumably, wishing to have that position in which he can gain most applause by contributing most to the common success. The aims of the individual and of the whole are the same.

There is a great deal of truth and encouragement in this view; it sets forth in one of its aspects the ideal towards which competition should aspire. We ought to strive for this state of things, and we can approach if not attain it. But the ascertained principles of evolution, as I understand them, will by no means permit us to assume a perfect natural adaptation between men and society. The fact seems to be rather, that the social order, continually changing, makes ever new and more trying demands upon humanity; that men, from the point of view of social organization, are to be looked upon as a mass of rough material, all of which is more or less imperfect, and some part of which, a part that might be greatly diminished by better husbandry, is unavailable. This part must be

[10] Emerson, "Essay on Greatness."

separated out and the remainder must be planed, sawed and tried here and there until fitted, with a view to getting the most use out of it with the least waste. A ready-made fit is quite exceptional. Each of us is fitter for some places than for others; but no one is fit for anything without a course of education and discipline, whose purpose is to produce an adaptation to social existence for which nature, at most, supplies only the undeveloped capacity.

It can hardly be necessary to argue at length that competition, however defective, does the work better than *status,* and that the real question of practical moment is that of increasing its efficiency. In this direction there is everything to be done; and the means, speaking generally, is the development of rational organization in every form, and particularly in the form of special selective agencies, chiefly educational, to supplement and in part to replace the somewhat blind and irrational competition that accompanies rapid change. It is a question of the quality of competition rather than of its quantity. The selective process should begin farther back, in an intelligent and truly free system of education, opening to every child opportunity and incitement to find out and pursue that career for which he is naturally best suited. The principle of *status* now persists in the too mechanical uniformity of education, and in its general failure to supply appropriate special training to the great mass of the people. The rising demand for a greater individualization in schools, for special study of each child with a view to making the most of him and teaching him how to make the most of himself, for manual training and trade schools accessible to all, is a demand for a more rational and open competition. In the lack of these things children, who need freedom most, are not free, but bound by the condition of their parents, and by the habits and ideas which they contract from their early associates and surroundings. Freedom is a positive and not a negative thing; it is to be secured not by mere letting alone, which is often abandonment to enslaving social conditions, but by rational social agencies deliberately organized to secure it.

True freedom, healthy organization and the highest type of competition inevitably go together; they are, indeed, various aspects of the same thing. Freedom is possible only through open competition and through an organization that promotes the highest development of each individual: the best organization is not only the outcome of rational freedom and just competition, but is also a means of securing these; in other words, the whole social structure and process is an organic whole which can be bettered only by a general advance all along the line.

Our time, as already suggested, is one in which, old social structures having gone to pieces, we are slowly and tentatively building up new ones. In the meantime the social process is at once intensified by the extraordinary call upon it and somewhat confused and demoralized by the failure of the structures which normally control and direct it. Our cities, especially, are full of the disintegrated material of the old order looking for a place in the new: men without trades, immigrants with alien habits and traditions, country boys and girls who have broken loose from their families and from early ties and beliefs, college graduates ignorant of the intellectual progress of the past fifty years, young theologians whose creeds the world has ceased to believe, and so on. There is no adequate means of dealing with this refractory material. Some of it is quite spoiled, and the moral and educational agencies, the customs, standards, traditions, associations and laws, required to assimilate the rest to the needs of the situation, cannot be created in a moment. In such a state of things competition becomes the immediate occasion of a great sum of misplacement, confusion and suffering, for which nothing but the situation as a whole is responsible.

The charge that it is a failure as an organizing process, that it puts the round men in the square holes and *vice versa,* causing dissatisfaction to individuals and detriment to society, will appear true or false according to the point of view from which one regards actual conditions. If one holds that each man is by nature fitted to perform some special function in the social system, that there is always something waiting to be done that he can do better than anybody else, and in doing which he finds his own happiness; if one blinks the difficulty of finding out just what this special function is, of educating the faculties to perform it, and of making a way through the throng to the place where it is to be performed; then he will be likely to pass a severe judgment upon the existing order, in which there are many total failures and innumerable misfits. But if he does justice to the difficulty of the problem, rejects as unsound the theory of perfect natural adaptation of men to functions, and compares competition, even in its present form, with the working of the alternative principle of *status,* he will easily discover much good that we must hold on to, as well as much ill that we must try to cast off.

There is no clear dividing line between individual and group competition. In a certain sense it may be said that there is no individual competition, since the competing person always draws aid and support of one sort or another from other persons. So far as a man is social and not merely animal, he is the center, and in a manner the product, of a complex web of relations and influences from which he can in no way be separated, unless by death. By "group," however, is ordinarily intended, in this connection, a definite association with distinct purposes and organization.

One of the chief purposes of the creation of such definite groups is to compete more effectually. They are tools devised by men to further their personal aims; and so far as the aims thus furthered meet with opposition, the group becomes a competing agency.

The main differences between a person as a competing unit and an organized group are the greater power and permanence that the latter may have, and its impersonality, the fact that, as is said of corporations, it "has no soul." Its action is not necessarily conditioned by that psychological unity of the various elements of human nature that exists in a person. In joining to create a social mechanism for the achievement of some special aim, such as exploiting a mine or electing a candidate to public office, a man isolates a certain part of himself, a certain wish or purpose, and sends it off by itself, so to speak, to work independently of the rest of his aims and impulses. Other men do the same and the result is essentially mechanical, and not human. The man, as a moral whole, is not in it; it is only a faggot of parallel interests. The man extends his reach, but in doing so he loses immediate control of the organ, and with that is likely to go all vivid sense of responsibility. The action of an organization is not necessarily lower morally than that of the individual men who create it, but it is likely to be; it is not so accessible to control by sentiment, by public opinion, by pride, vanity, and other peculiarly human influences. As members of a corporation, a legislature or a party, men will share in doing things which they would not do if they were to be held personally responsible for them. It is also true that as members of philanthropical and educational organizations men frequently build better than they know, better than they seriously or continuously intend.

The fact that definite associations are more numerous and more specialized than they have been in the past increases this impersonal tendency. This circumstance, which is connected with the increased facility of association effected by modern communication, brings it to pass that the modern man shares in many associations, each one of which is narrowly restricted in its aim, and of course feels a personal responsibility for each in inverse ratio to their number. The broader association of the past, for instance the medieval trade-guild, embracing almost the whole social, æsthetic and religious life of the individual, must have been a more *human* thing than the modern corporation or trades-union.

These two attributes of competing organizations, power and impersonality, together with the fact that they are, for the most part, new and unassimilated elements in the social system, entirely justify the expectation that they will require special and somewhat stringent means of control. All forms of power must be controlled and subordinated to the general life and aims; freedom means not the diminution of such subordination and control but the substitution of higher forms for lower, the replacing of tradition, authority and *status* by something that works upon intelligent choice through appeals to feeling or principle. Organized groups being comparatively little amenable to these higher forms of control must be correspondingly subjected to the lower, that is to legal restrictions: being impersonal they cannot share fully in the growth of personal freedom.

An important and substantially new problem is thus introduced into political science by the rapid rise of powerful and highly-specialized private associations. In the past it has been the policy, I believe, of all stable governments to control strictly, if not to repress, organizations formed independently of them. This is still largely the case outside of the United States and Great Britain. There is no freedom of association in Russia; and little in France or Germany compared with what we enjoy. In the United States the legal presumption is, and should be, in favor of the beneficence or harmlessness of all exercise of private initiative until it appears by experience to be harmful. Where harmfulness does appear, the question before our jurists and legislators is, just what control is required and how may it best be applied? The matter is greatly complicated by the fact that not only are the forms of association new and hard to manage, but the industries themselves, which the associations carry on, are largely new also, and would require a new body of law simply as industries, even if they were carried on by individuals. Thus, in connection with railways we have two distinct classes of questions: the corporation problem, including what relates to the form of organization, questions common to this and to other great industries; and the railway problem proper, arising from the special nature of this particular industry.

The matter may be summed up by saying that, as before hinted, it is a question of symmetry in development. Urged on by the necessities of the situation, industrial activities, and the social relations arising from them, have far outstripped other activities which in a symmetrical social order should balance and control them. This fact is patent everywhere; it is the key to the whole situation. Law, religious belief, art, moral standards, have been left far behind; and the great need of the time is that they should catch up with the procession.

Owing to this backwardness of the means of control, group competition, even more than any other sort, is in a state of partial anarchy or border-ruffianism. These gigantic, unmoral creatures are restrained, if at all, rather by the primitive fear of retaliation than anything else. Things are in the fighting stage, which has not yet brought to light the conditions of equilibrium, and given place to that subordination to rule that characterizes an orderly society. . . .

THE STANDARD OF SUCCESS

Success, as I use the word, is whatever men think it is; that is to say it is nothing other than the achievement, or the hopeful pursuit, of the object of endeavor. Now the object of endeavor which each person sets before himself is, like all the products of our minds, at once individual and social in its origin. It represents the ideas concerning success offered by the social environment organized according to the structure of the individual mind. What I think worth doing must always be a function, more or less involved, of what other people think, or have thought, worth doing. It is therefore no denial of individuality to say that the object of endeavor reflects the sentiment of the social group, and that there is for every group, for every nation and every age, a standard of success more or less peculiar and characteristic. So far as life is determined by the animal necessities, to exist and propagate is success; but beyond this point, when this primary object is secured and a surplus of energy remains, success begins to take on a social or moral character and the object striven for becomes more and more the production of some effect upon the minds of others, the achievement of respect, honor, power, love, or beneficence. These are clearly the chief objects of endeavor in existing society, under normal conditions. The literal "struggle for existence" comes into painful prominence at times, but on the whole it plays only a small part. What this expression really means in most cases is the struggle to maintain what is called a standard of living; and this is altogether a social or psychological phenomenon. Our standard of living is fixed by what others think, by what those whose respect we wish to retain regard as decent and necessary. It is one thing while a man is at home, and quite a different thing when he is upon a hunting trip. It is determined by his habit of thought and his social environment. The more aggressive forms of ambition, which engage those who are not content with merely maintaining a standard of living, have also this social and imaginative character. The objects sought are power, reputation, beneficence; always the production of some desired effect upon the minds of other persons.

Wealth as an object of ambition and a measure of success owes its ascendency to its social implications, and the pursuit of it is by no means a proof of materialism or sensuality. Wealth is merely a symbol for the power into which it is convertible, and for the sake of which it is desired. The fact that a man desires it, throws little or no light upon the real object of his ambition. He may want it to pamper his stomach, to build a fine house, to further his political ambition, or to carry on a social settlement. Of these, however they may differ in ethical value, the first alone is a material or

sensual aim. The rest are social and look to the minds of others for
their success. As regards mere sensualism, it would seem that it
does not play and never has played any very important part as an
object of ambition. It does not appeal to that social imagination
which is the basis of all ambition. Men may become sensualists
after they achieve wealth—though that is usually left for the heirs
—but sensual pleasure was not the object for which they strove.
They sought wealth in order to have power, and the respect and
admiration which power commands; or, as I think is usually the
case, simply because they needed to strive for something and this
was the object that most readily presented itself. They sought
what they found others seeking, just to be in the game. The more
ambition one has, even of the more selfish sorts, the less he is likely
to fall into sensuality.

It may seem to some that this assertion that ambition is essentially social, and that its object is the production of some desired
effect upon the minds of others, is contradicted by the fact that
rich and successful men often display a great contempt for what
others think, and openly "trample upon the moral sentiment of
the people." I think, however, that a close scrutiny of the facts will
show that this supposed contempt of public opinion seldom or
never exists. If it does exist, it is simply because the person in
question looks for the gratification of his ambition to the minds
of some small group: his rivals and associates in business, perhaps,
whose sentiment differs from that of the public in general. The
truth, in most cases, is that the opinion or moral sentiment disregarded is that of only a small part—though very possibly the best
part—of the community. It is disregarded largely because attention
is fixed upon the majority, who are indifferent to the actions rep-
robated and are ready to admire wealth and power however obtained. In seeking these things our rich men, our plutocrats if you
will, are simply conforming to the reigning conception of what
constitutes success.

Because it is a symbol convertible into any one of many forms
of power, wealth must always be a main object of endeavor, and
its attainment will perhaps remain for a majority of persons, the
accepted standard of success. There seems to be a truth, however,
in the idea that it plays a larger part than it should at the present

time; larger, perhaps, than it has ordinarily played in the past. The kinds of power which wealth assures are after all the lower kinds. It will buy material commodities, mechanical service, and plenty of a certain sort of admiration. But the finer, stronger and more generous spirits among men are not, as a rule, to be satisfied with these; they crave something more ideal, more enduring, more personal, some higher place in the minds of those with whom they sympathize, something that, as I said above, appeals more to the social imagination. Ambitions of this higher sort are to be gratified by creative work in literature or art, by heroic deeds upon the field of battle or elsewhere, by eloquence in any noble cause, by the sort of philanthropy that involves personal service, and so on.

As compared with these finer ambitions, the pursuit of wealth now absorbs more of the endeavor of the higher class of minds than has commonly been the case in the past. The dazzling succession of inventions and the sequent material progress have had a semihypnotic effect in turning the attention of men in this one direction and in shutting it off from others. The work at hand has been material work, chiefly the development of new means of production. Men have taken it up, and with the emulation inseparable from human energy have striven with one another to excel in it and to gain the power and honor that goes with success. But in such work, more than in others, the accumulation of wealth is the proof and symbol of success; and this, accordingly, has more and more become the accepted standard, even for a sort of minds that in another state of things would have risen above it. A standard or type of success, set-a-going in this way, tends strongly to perpetuate itself. It becomes established in the habit of thought, in public sentiment, tradition and education, while other standards or types are neglected. Children are brought up in it; it is in the air; this comes to seem real and solid while other ideals are looked upon as vague and visionary. A few hundred years ago it seemed the most natural thing in the world to the ambitious among our ancestors, to sell off their property, raise a company and set off to the Holy Land to rescue it from the infidels. This is incomprehensible to us, but we see nothing strange in a man of ambition and imagination devoting a lifetime of strenuous endeavor to the making of tubs or the organized slaughter of hogs. One of these aims is no more strange than the other; both are natural and human, and the men who will do the one thing in one age are very probably the same who would do the other in another age.

We must, then, conclude that the standard of success which our age presses most strongly upon our attention is a narrow and, in some sense, a low one. It needs to be raised and diversified. The standard of success should be the symmetrical reflection of all the needs of human nature, not the exaggerated image of a few of them. Without expecting that wealth will cease to be an object of pretty general esteem and endeavor, we may hope and strive to break down the ascendency which it exercises over a class of persons who would serve the world better and find more happiness for themselves if they could devote their energies to the discovery of truth, the creation of beauty, or some other of the more imaginative aims. It may be asked, what is to hinder? The answer, however, is not difficult: to undertake careers of this sort in the face of the indifference to them which for the most part prevails, requires a self-confidence and vigor of initiative which is rare; the special education necessary is often unattainable; the chance of making a living is not encouraging; and, most fatal of all by far, the state of public sentiment denies to the follower of art, for example, that appreciative sympathy which is essential to the unfolding of talent. The present age acts upon a large class of minds of the finer order as an uncongenial climate acts upon a plant: it chills them and stunts their growth: they feel homesick. And, aside from these, people in general would be much the better for the broader and richer life which a widening of the field of endeavor would bring with it.

To attempt to point out in detail just how this raising and diversification of the standard is to be effected would carry us too far from our special topic: it would simply lead out to a general discussion of social tendencies and the means of progress. I may say, however, that here, as elsewhere, the method of betterment is a vigorous exercise of individual energy and self-reliance. Each innovating individual, so far as he makes his ideas valid, alters the standard of success, opens new opportunities, does something toward the general upbuilding of the social structure.

It will be apparent, I think, that the view regarding the nature of success here maintained is decidedly a hopeful one so far as concerns the possibility of progress, and wholly opposed to the pessimistic attitude based on the supposed "selfishness" of human nature and inevitable predominance of the economic motive. The motive that really predominates, now as in the past, is essentially social and moral; it is the desire to be something in the minds of others, to gain respect, honor, social power of some sort. This being the case, human endeavor is above all things plastic, controlled by the spirit of the age. The standard of success, and with it the whole character and tendency of competition, is a social or moral phenomenon accessible to human endeavor. Society can and does determine what success is.

The System of Social Control

EDWARD ALSWORTH ROSS

Edward Alsworth Ross (1866–1951) was born in Virden, Illinois, and grew up in Iowa. He graduated from Coe College and was granted his Ph.D. in economics by Johns Hopkins. His teaching career, after a year each at Indiana and Cornell, took him to Stanford. Forced out of that institution because of his views, he taught for five years at the University of Nebraska before going to Wisconsin in 1906, where he remained as professor of sociology until his retirement in 1937. His scholarly output included several hundred articles and twenty-eight books. He was elected president of the American Sociological Association in 1914 and re-elected in 1915. The following selection is part of an article in the *American Journal of Sociology*, III (1898); the article in turn is the thirteenth installment in a series by Ross on "Social Control" which ran at intervals in the first four volumes of this periodical.

I.

IF A NUMBER of institutions that mutually determine each other may be said to form a system, then we may properly speak of "the system of social control." Certainly there is a division of labor tending to assign to each form of control that work for which it is best fitted. Law concerns itself with that undesirable conduct which is at once important and capable of clear definition. Central positive qualities—courage or veracity in man, chastity in woman —are taken in charge by the sense of honor or self-respect. The religious sanction is ordinarily reserved for those acts and abstinences requiring the utmost backing. Religion mounts guard

151

over the ancient, unvarying fundamentals of group life, but deals little with the temporary adjustments required from time to time. The taking of life or property, adultery, unfilial conduct, and false swearing encounter its full force; but not adulteration, stock gambling, or corporation frauds. In code as in ritual and belief religion betrays its archaic character.

In morals as well as in microscopes we have a major and a minor adjusting apparatus. In adaptability public opinion stands at one end of a series of which religion is the other extreme. Connected with this is a gradation in the nature of the sanction. Public opinion bans many things not unlawful, law may require much more than self-respect, and self-respect may be wounded by that which is not regarded as sinful. But the universality of the sanction grows as the scope of prohibition narrows. In the first case the offender encounters the public here and now, in the second the crystallized disapproval of society, in the third the opinion of generations of men who have conspired to frame a standard or ideal, and in the last case the frown of the Ruler of the Universe.

The champions of each detail of regulation strive, therefore, to get these successive sanctions behind their commandments. The opponents of drinking, dancing, divorce, usury, horseracing, dueling, speculation, or prize fighting, strive to make the practices first blameworthy, then unlawful, then shameful, and finally sinful. But this massing of sanctions is very naturally resisted. The attempt to get God against a new vice, such as liquor selling, always encounters fierce opposition from those who find themselves suddenly shut out from the odor of sanctity. New moral tests, like new party tests, endanger ground already won, and so imperil the sanctions for the major virtues. It is not well, therefore, to associate loss of honor with white lies or the Divine Displeasure with card playing. Sympathy, religious sentiment, self-respect, sense of duty, fear, regard for public opinion, enlightened self-interest— each has its place and its task, and no one motive should be overworked.

The community draws no firm line between what offends it and what harms it. The ideals held up for imitation include table manners as well as honesty. Public disapproval must be faced by the non-conforming freethinker or dress-reformer as well as the swin-

dler and the traitor. Religion claims its holy days and its fasts as
well as just dealings. At times even the law becomes the instrument
of a tyrannous majority. Codes, standards, and moral distinctions
have crystallized out of collective feeling, and they will not draw a
sharp line between public and private conduct unless collective
feeling concerns itself exclusively with the collective interest. But
this never occurs. The common resentment is never warden merely
of the common welfare, but busies itself with sacrilege, profanity,
sodomy, or cruelty to animals. It is thus that society comes to put
its sanction behind the rules of private living, and even behind
useless injunctions.

The margin of social control is a fluctuating margin. Just as law
is always dying at some points and growing at others, so the requirements of public opinion or religion are ever changing. Society,
while relinquishing its control over a man's Sundays, his church
connections, his clothes, and his expletives, is just beginning to
regulate his treatment of his children, his drinking habits, and his
expenditure on elections. The running of a scientific frontier between the individual and society is the joint task of two contrasted
types of thought. The eighteenth-century philosophy, ardent for
the individual, sought to draw about each man the largest possible
inviolable circle. On all laws, restraints, moral requirements, and
duties needlessly invading this circle, it has kept up a steady fire
of criticism and remonstrance. Nineteenth-century thought, on the
other hand, convinced that if there be no God, King, State, Moral
Order, or Scheme of Things to serve as fountain head of obligations, there is at least a Social Interest, has been diligent to show
all hidden and unsuspected ways in which the interest of many is
harmed by this or that exercise of power. Consequently it has become sponsor for a multitude of new commandments and duties.
These two tendencies have not resulted in deadlock, as some
imagine, but in a thorough overhauling and testing of every detail
of restraint which will result, let us hope, in giving us the most
welfare for the least abridgment of liberty.

Changes in knowledge, in degree of civilization, and in the character of social requirements cause a method of control to wax or
wane from age to age. We might compare the social order to a
viaduct across some wooded ravine in the Sierras which rests part

of its weight on timbers that decay with the lapse of time, and part on living tree trunks which constantly gain in strength. Or we might liken it to a bridge resting on piers built, some of stone which crumbles in time, and some of stone which hardens with long exposure to the air. No doubt etiquette and ceremony have done their best work. The seer of visions and dreamer of dreams has had his day. The hero will never again be the pivot of order. The reign of custom with its vague terrors is about over. The assizes of Osiris, Rhadamanthus, God, or Allah, with their books of record, inquisitions, and judgments, will hardly dominate the imagination in the days to come. The reputed dispensations of Providence will less and less affect conduct. A fictive blood kinship cannot bind men into the national groups of today. So public action in the form of mob, ban, or boycott is justly regarded as a relic of barbarism.

On the other hand, instruction as to the consequences of actions, with a view to enlisting an enlightened self-interest in support of all the conduct it is competent to sanction, will meet with universal approval in an age of public education; and the passiveness of the average mind will make it safe to work into such moral instruction certain convenient illusions and fallacies which it is nobody's interest to denounce. Suggestion, that little understood instrument, will no doubt be found increasingly helpful in establishing moral imperatives in the young. But it will render its greatest service in shaping in youth those feelings of admiration or loathing that determine the ruling ideals of character, and in influencing those imputations of worth which enable society to impose upon the individual its own valuations of life's activities and experiences. And society will further the work by cutting with cameo-like clearness the types of character it chooses to commend, and by settling ever more firmly, in tradition and convention, the values it seeks to impose. But from social art we have the most to look for. I would place it next to religion in power to transform the brute into the angel. Art is one of the few moral instruments which, instead of being blunted by the vast changes in opinion, have gained edge and sweep by these very changes. So far as eye can pierce the future, there is nothing to limit or discredit it. The sympathies it fosters do not, it is true, establish norms and duties; but they lift that plane of general sentiment out of which imperatives and obligations arise. If there is anyone in this age who does the work of the Isaiahs and Amoses of old, it is an Ibsen, a Tolstoi, a Victor Hugo, or a Thomas Hardy.

II

It is a mistake to suppose there will be less need in the future for society to dominate the souls of its members. On the contrary, we may expect the more far-reaching and pervasive means of control, such as suggestion, ideals, and social valuations, to be used in the twentieth century much more freely and consciously than they now are. The ground for such belief is the visible disruption of the *community* and the rise of *society* as claimant of all allegiances and object of all duties. So far as *community* extends, people naturally keep themselves orderly, and there is no call to put them under the yoke of an elaborate discipline. The sense of a common life that grows up in the family, the kindred, the neighborhood, the circle of companions, or the band of comrades, leads relatives, neighbors and mates to love and understand one another, to yield one to another, and to observe those forbearances and offices that make associate life a success. To people abiding in such natural relations the apparatus of control appears as an impediment and an impertinence. The reaction of man against man and a kind of reciprocal constraint will, of course, show itself among kinsmen and neighbors; but of control, formal and organized, there will be little sign.

Now these natural bonds are ceasing to bind men as men must be bound in the aggregates of today. Kinship has lost its sacred significance and binding force. Social erosion has reduced the family to parents and young. Marriage has become a contract, terminable almost at pleasure. Nearness of dwelling means little in the country and nothing in the town. To the intimacy of the countryside succeeds the "multitudinous desolation" of the city. The workingman has become a bird of passage. Touch-and-go acquaintanceship takes the place of those lasting attachments that form between neighbors who have lived, labored, and holidayed together.

It is true that, while the local group dissolves, new forms of union arise. Friendship is freer, and hence firmer; and there are bonds of fellowship growing up between co-religionists, fellow-craftsmen, or people of the same social class. But these forms of social feeling repose not on blood or nearness or intercourse, but on personal preference. They are after the manner of friendship which implies freedom and choice. The new forms of spontaneous association, as they imply a preference of some over others, do not embrace all those of a given place, or who have dealings one with another. Consequently they do not foster that community spirit which is the natural support of restraints and duties. We dare not establish obligation upon one of these special feelings; for the circle of obligation must be as wide as the circle of contacts, else order fails and the community perishes of partisanship or class feeling or religious hatreds.

It is not to be denied that sympathy has gained in range and that there is now a civic, national, or racial community binding men into groups much larger than the Semitic "tribe," the Greek "city," the Teutonic "kindred," the medieval "town," or the New World "settlement." But these new communities are not tissues formed of the interlacing tendrils of individual lives. They are born of effort and maintained by the use of appropriate means. Civic pride and public spirit are often hothouse plants, and we see patriotism, the specific bond of the national community, openly fostered by art, ceremony, ideal, and symbol. We must face the fact, therefore, that the *community*, undermined by the stream of change, has caved in, carrying with it part of the foundations of order. While not overlooking that growth of intelligence which, by enabling us to comprehend large bodies of people at a distance, invites fellowship to overleap the limits of personal contact, I am bound to say that we are relying on artificial rather than natural supports to bear the increasing weight of our social order, and that a return to a natural basis of social partnership seems about as unlikely as a return to natural food or natural locomotion.

The reader may shudder at the thought of modern society precariously rearing its huge bulk above the devouring waves of selfishness like a Venice built on piles. But it is perhaps no worse than man's depending on cultivated instead of wild fruits, or removing the seats of his civilization to climates where only artificial heat can keep alive through the winter. So long as there is bread and

coal enough, what matters our dependence on art! And so long
as society can stamp its standards and values on its members, what
matters our dependence on forms of control!

Not that the future is secure. The crash may yet come through
the strife of classes, each unable to master the others by means of
those influences that subdue the individual. But if it comes, it will
be due to the mal-distribution of wealth effected by new, blind,
economic forces we have not learned to regulate, and will no more
discredit the policy of social control than the failure of the mountain reservoir discredits irrigation.

III

From the recorded social experience of five thousand years it
ought to be possible to draw true criteria for judging a method of
control. Even our brief reconnaissance enables us to declare that
the marks of a good disciplinary agent include the following:

Economy. On this principle, a method that molds character is
superior to one that deals merely with conduct, the symptom or
index of character. A roundabout way, such as the imparting of
social valuations, is preferable to the direct method of playing
upon hopes and fears. A farsighted policy, such as the training of
the young, excels the summary regulation of the adult. In the concrete these maxims mean that the priest is often cheaper than the
policeman, the school costs less than the prison, and the Sunday
school saves at Botany Bay. And accordingly we can recommend
the salutation of the flag in the army to the court-martial, prefer a
little reform school for the boy to much jail for the man, and
declare it better to reform the offender, once we have him, than to
catch and convict him again.

Inwardness. Sanction operates only so long as it is sure. Let
witnesses be wanting or authority weak, and the ill will issues in
deed. Consequently the control of the will by suggestion is to be
preferred to control of the will by hopes and fears; and a flank
movement aiming to influence feelings and judgments is better
tactics than a direct assault on the volitions. The lodgment of a
social ideal in the soul's inner citadel gives a steadier ascendency
than assemblage, festival, public worship, or ceremony at stated
occasions. An impression upon the judgment is worth more than

an effervescent sentiment, such as is evoked by music. But moral precepts that seduce the judgment by masquerading as worldly wisdom may not always be relied on either. They bind a man in so far as his choices are ruled by rational considerations; but plays and tales will never tire of showing the pet maxims of reasonable conduct swept aside by imperious instincts, passions, and emotions.

The best guarantee of a stable control from within is something that will reach at once sentiment, reason, and will. Consequently a religion is widely effective for righteousness in so far as it is strong in these three directions. It should strike the chord of feeling, but not so exclusively as Quakerism, or Shinto, or the Religion of Humanity, or Neo-Catholicism. It should teach a day of reckoning, but not dwell on it so much as Islam or primitive Methodism. It should address the judgment, but not become so baldly rational as the English church in the time of Tillotson. The secret of the limited habitat of certain sects is found in a narrowness of appeal that restricts them to certain temperaments or certain social layers.

Simplicity of belief basis. Elements of conviction are, of course, associated with most forms of control. But when a type of restraint rests squarely on an unverifiable dogma, such as the Last Judgment, the Unseen Friend, or the Divine Fatherhood, it must be regarded askance, however transcendent its services. Either the dogma crumbles, and with it the restraint, leaving the last state of a man worse than the first; or else the dogma obstinately kept as a moral fulcrum becomes a stumbling-block to enlightenment, a bar to progress, a shelter to superstition, and an offense to that intellectual honesty and sincerity which is one of the most precious instincts of the modern man. But of course dogmas differ vastly both in their value to morals and their harm to science.

Decentralized management. It is bad for the enginery of discipline to lie in the hands of a small part of society, an élite, class, caste, or profession. In some cases this may be necessary in order to curb and civilize a backward many. But we have only to recall the despotism of Druids, Brahmins, Magi, Spanish priests, Scotch ministers, and New England parsons to see that the few will always push their interferences to excess. Moreover, the wielding of the instruments of power gives an opportunity for personal or class aggrandizement that is rarely neglected. Provided the dominant few are well organized or knit together, their class egoism is bound to assert itself. Witness the riches, exemptions, and license of the medieval Catholic hierarchy. So a vast administrative system holding in order a heterogeneous people is sure to become a screen for aggrandizement. But it is when the official and ecclesiastical hierarchies work together, as under Henry VIII, Philip II, Louis XIV, or Nicholas II, that the exploitation feature becomes most noticeable.

There is always danger that the desiderata of joint life will be lost sight of in the zeal to make men over by the clever manipulation of powerful influences. Thus the Quixotic ideal of "one language, one church, one government," too ardently pursued, leads Russia into high-handed persecution of Raskolniks and Stundists. The exuberance of fanatics and pietists must be checked and naked righteousness held up as the one thing needful. Those who command the machinery of church and state come to entertain large designs for dominating the mind with dogma and priestcraft, gag and censor; but these ambitious designs to make men as bricks are turned out of the mold can be frustrated by the *diffusion of control*.

Professor Burgess has shown[1] how *individual liberty* had to be recognized and organized into the state as well as *government*. Now it is equally necessary that in the moral sphere liberty should get so intrenched as to offer stout resistance to all excessive control. The moral individualism that follows like a shadow the continuing aggregation of mankind into larger wholes testifies to the need of a brake on moral centralization. In the little tribe or city-state of antiquity, the social spirit ruled unquestioned, and the open cult of the individual would have been like touching off a powder magazine. But with far-flung dominion, elaborate religions, organized priesthoods, and vast school systems designed to impose ready-made formulae, the man is liable to be held too firmly in the network. The ascendency of society becomes easy and hence dangerous. Lawmaker, official, priest, parson, schoolmaster, master of ceremonies, or moral philosopher exact much more than they

[1] In his *Political Science and Comparative Constitutional Law,* Vol. I.

need to ask for. On behalf of God or prince, neighbor or group, one is called upon to give up the most that makes life worth the living. Accordingly, freedom becomes a passion, *laissez faire* a dogma, skepticism a religion, and all the rills of opposition run together into a great current of opposition, which accompanies the development of control as a check and a reminder.

Worse than the strait-jacket of the Pharisee is the warping of human nature with moral appliances. To get stern self-discipline it is necessary to split up the soul into the acting self and the watching self. But this means the loss of that wholesome unconsciousness and outlook which is the birthright of healthy beings. The conscientious man is a kind of degenerate. The heart-searching, spirit-wrestling self-examination that is fostered by all moralizing schemes may help multitudes to a better life, but it is not the crown and roof of the human spirit. To him who has arrived at frank, communal feeling the groanings and wrestlings, the Puritan conscience, the sin notion, the fussiness of the moral novice, will perhaps become, like the whip and hair shirt, mere memories of a bad dream. And in his "eventual element of calm" he may echo the sentiment of Walt Whitman:

I think I could turn and live with animals, they are so placid and
    self-contain'd,
They do not sweat and whine about their condition,
They do not lie awake in the dark and weep for their sins,
They do not make me sick discussing their duty to God,
Not one is dissatisfied, not one is demented with the mania of owning
    things,
Not one kneels to another or to one of his kind that lived thousands
    of years ago,
Not one is respectable or unhappy over the whole earth.[2]

IV

To expose the antinomy that lies at the foundation of society and to show faiths, moralities, and wisdom, in all their nakedness as so many ways of luring a man from the pursuit of his private welfare is to subvert all control save that of force. "In vain in the sight of the bird the net of the fowler is spread." One who learns why society is urging him into the strait and narrow way will

---

[2] *Leaves of Grass,* "Song of Myself."

resist its pressure. One who sees clearly the method of control will thenceforth be emancipated. Of course he may cleave to goodness and justice—and they are not exotic to human nature —but no one knowingly consents to be controlled. To betray the secrets of social ascendency is to forearm the individual in his struggle with society. If at the hour that now strikes the Anglo-Saxon is overregulated, his conscience too sensitive, his ideals too imperious, his conduct too devoted, his proper development checked, then let us show him the net in which he is taken. But if he still thwarts his fellows more than our control thwarts him, let us beware of rashly strengthening an individualism already too rampant.

Since the days of Reimarus and Priestley bold scientific analysis has destroyed vicious forms of control guarded by darkness and superstition, till it has become an acknowledged axiom that all dissections may take place in public. It is now an article of faith that truth can never harm and cannot be proclaimed too widely. When human action is seen to be influenced by baseless faiths or wrong ideas, it has been assumed that we cannot too quickly foster doubt and question. But this optimism has prevailed simply because the iconoclasm of natural science could do little harm so long as the veil was not lifted from those sacred recesses where are prepared the convictions and sentiments by which society holds together. Science, like Bishop Blougram, might "cut and cut again," but found "ever a next in size now grown as big."

But rising sociology will put to the test this childlike faith in the naked truth. When we learn the sources of the Nile flood of idealism that makes the desert to blossom with virtues, when we behold those mysterious processes that take place in the soul of a people, when the products of the social mind are split up into their elements, we shall realize, no doubt, what it is that holds men together. And when the hour of illumination comes, will the social scientist lightheartedly assail every conviction or ideal he cannot rationalize? Will not the loyal investigator hesitate to send the tell-tale carmine stain into every filament that helps hold the individual in the mesh of unsuspected influences?

The secret of order is, therefore, not to be bawled from every housetop. The fact of control is no gospel to be preached abroad

with allegory and parable, with bold type and scare headlines. The
social investigator will show religion a consideration it has rarely
met with in the natural scientist. He will venerate the moral
system too much to uncover its nakedness. He will speak to men,
not to youth. He will address himself to those who administer the
moral capital of society: to teachers, clergymen, editors, law-
makers, and judges, who wield the instruments of control; to
poets, artists, thinkers, and educators, who are the guides of the
human caravan. Some may scent danger in a science keeping
itself half esoteric. But surely the men of widest horizon and
farthest vision who, making the joint welfare their own, wage
perpetual war against predatory appetite, greedy ambition, un-
blushing impudence, and brutal injustice, may safely be intrusted
with the secrets of control! When control ceases to be necessary,
we can tell the "recruity," the street Arab, and the Elmira "inmate"
how it was done. Until then, discretion!

v

I cannot too strongly urge the study of moral influences by the
right persons and in the right spirit as a basis for a scientific control
of the individual. The foundations of order must be laid completely bare ere we can wisely go about to broaden or underpin
them. Many great thinkers have begun the task, but in their
eagerness to have this pier strengthened or that pillar kept, they
have failed to make a thorough exploration. In his *Republic,*
Plato has given perhaps the best review of the conditions of order.
But Machiavelli uttered certain of its secrets. Rousseau fingered
the springs of social feeling. Burke laid down the requisites of
stability. Napoleon told how men are governed. Carlyle demon-
strated the value of persons. Mazzini preached the efficacy of
ideals. Horace Mann championed the worth of enlightenment.
Victor Hugo showed what society owes to art. Guyeau pointed
out the power of suggestion. Ibsen reminds of the curative value
of freedom. But too often each has declared his own the corner-
stone and reviled those who found solidity in some other prop or
buttress. And society, distracted by the cries of partisans, has
excitedly torn down or hastily built up the various supports of its
order with little rational idea of what it was doing.

The social system of control has been a dark jungle harboring warring bands of guerrillas; but when investigators with the scientific method have fully occupied this region, the disorder and dacoity ought to cease. Surely there must be some general principles from the vantage ground of which to pass upon the conflicting pretensions of drill sergeant and anarchist, of authoritarian and suasionist, of priest and schoolmaster, of censor and artist, of Jesuit and freethinker, of tory and radical, of prude and Adamite, of moral philosopher and evolutionist. And these we shall get when an exploration of the subject shall show how many modes and instruments of social control there are, and enable us to appraise each at its true value. As soon as the conditions which reconcile order with progress are made clear to the leaders of opinion, the control of society over its members ought to become more conscious and effective than it now is, and the dismal seesawing between change and reaction that has been the curse of this century ought to disappear. . . .

The Issue

EUGENE V. DEBS

Eugene V. Debs (1855–1926) was born of French immigrant parents in Terre Haute, Indiana, and lived there all his life. As a youth he worked as a locomotive fireman; after he quit the railroads he was active in the Brotherhood of Locomotive Firemen, serving as national secretary-treasurer and editor of its magazine. He resigned in 1892 and the next year helped form the American Railway Union. In spite of unprecedented successes, the ARU was destroyed in the violent Pullman strike of 1894. Debs turned to socialism, and for a generation he was the country's foremost agitator for a sweeping reorganization of society. Much of his influence came from his articles in the *Appeal to Reason,* which was mailed each week to some 300,000 subscribers from the little town of Girard in southeastern Kansas. Debs gave this impromptu talk at a street fair in Girard on May 23, 1908, just after the Socialist party had named him for the third time as its candidate for President. From Bruce Rogers, editor, *Debs: His Life, Writings and Speeches* (1908).

COMRADES, Ladies and Gentlemen: . . . I am a new resident of Girard; have been here but a comparatively short time, and yet I feel myself as completely at home among you, most of whom disagree with me upon very vital questions, as I do in the town in which I was born and reared and have lived all the days of my life. Since the day I first came here I have been treated with uniform kindness. I could not have been treated more hospitably anywhere. I have met practically all of your people, and all of them have taken me by the hand and treated me as cordially as if I had been neighbor and friend with them; and to say that I appreciate this is to express myself in hackneyed and unsatisfactory terms.

The honor to which reference has been made has come to me through no fault of my own. It has been said that some men are born great, some achieve greatness, and some have greatness thrust upon them. It is even so with what are called honors. Some men have honors thrust upon them. I find myself in that class. I did what little I could to prevent myself from being nominated by the convention now in session at Chicago, but the nomination sought me out, and in spite of myself I stand in your presence this afternoon the nominee of the Socialist party for the presidency of the United States.

Long, long ago I made up my mind never again to be a candidate for any political office within the gift of the people. I was constrained to violate that vow because when I joined the Socialist party I was taught that the desire of the individual was subordinate to the party will, and that when the party commanded it was my duty to obey. There was a time in my life when I had the vanities of youth, when I sought that bubble called fame. I have outlived it. I have reached that point when I am capable of placing an estimate upon my own relative insignificance. I have come to realize that there is no honor in any real sense of that term to any man unless he is capable of freely consecrating himself to the service of his fellow men.

To the extent that I am able to help those who are unable to help themselves, to that extent, and to that extent alone, do I honor myself and the party to which I belong. So far as the presidency of the United States is concerned, I would spurn it were it not that it conferred the power to serve the working class, and he who enters that office with any other conception of it prostitutes and does not honor that office.

Now, my friends, I am opposed to the system of society in which we live today, not because I lack the natural equipment to do for myself, but because I am not satisfied to make myself comfortable knowing that there are thousands upon thousands of my fellow men who suffer for the barest necessities of life. We were taught under the old ethic that man's business upon this earth was to look out for himself. That was the ethic of the jungle;

the ethic of the wild beast. Take care of yourself, no matter what may become of your fellow man. Thousands of years ago the question was asked: "Am I my brother's keeper?" That question has never yet been answered in a way that is satisfactory to civilized society.

Yes, I am my brother's keeper. I am under a moral obligation to him that is inspired, not by any maudlin sentimentality, but by the higher duty I owe to myself. What would you think of me if I were capable of seating myself at a table and gorging myself with food and saw about me the children of my fellow beings starving to death?

Allow me to say to you, my fellow men, that nature has spread a great table bounteously for all of the children of men. There is room for all and there is a plate and a place and food for all, and any system of society that denies a single one the right and the opportunity to freely help himself to nature's bounties is an unjust and iniquitous system that ought to be abolished in the interest of a higher humanity and a civilization worthy of the name. And here let me observe, my fellow men, that while the general impression is that human society is stationary—a finality as it were—it is not so for a single instant. Underlying society there are great material forces that are in operation all of the circling hours of the day and night, and at certain points in the social development these forces outgrow the forms that hold them and these forms spring apart and then a new social system comes into existence and a new era dawns for the human race.

The great majority of mankind have always been in darkness. The overwhelming majority of the children of men have always been their own worst enemies. In every age of this world's history, the kings and emperors and czars and potentates, in alliance with the priests, have sought by all the means at their command to keep the people in darkness that they might perpetuate the power in which they riot and revel in luxury while the great mass are in a state of slavery and degradation, and he who has spoken out courageously against the existing order, he who has dared to voice the protest of the oppressed and downtrodden, has had to pay the penalty, all the way from Jesus Christ of Galilee down to Fred Warren of Girard.

Do you know, my friends, it is so easy to agree with the ignorant majority. It is so easy to make the people applaud an empty platitude. It takes some courage to face that beast called the Majority, and tell him the truth to his teeth! Some men do so and accept the consequences of their acts as becomes men, and they live in history—every one of them. I have said so often, and I wish to repeat it on this occasion, that mankind have always crowned their oppressors, and they have as uniformily crucified their saviors, and this has been true all along the highway of the centuries. It is true today. It will not always be so. When the great mass know the truth, they will treat an honest man decently while he lives and not crucify him, and then a thousand years afterward rear a monument above the dust of the hero they put to death.

I am in revolt against capitalism (and that doesn't mean to say, my friends, that I am hating you—not the slightest). I am opposed to capitalism because I love my fellow men, and if I am opposing you I am opposing you for what I believe to be your good, and though you spat upon me with contempt I should still oppose you to the extent of my power.

I don't hate the workingman because he has turned against me. I know the poor fellow is too ignorant to understand his self-interest, and I know that as a rule the workingman is the friend of his enemy and the enemy of his friend. He votes for men who represent a system in which labor is simply merchandise; in which the man who works the hardest and longest has the least to show for it.

If there is a man on this earth who is entitled to all the comforts and luxuries of this life in abundance it is the man whose labor produces them. If he is not, who is? Does he get them in the present system?

And, mark you, I am not speaking in a partisan sense this afternoon. I appreciate the fact that you have come here as Republicans and Democrats as well as Socialists to do me a personal honor, and I would be ungrateful, indeed, if I took advantage of such an occasion to speak to you in an offensive partisan sense. I wish to say in the broadest possible way that I am opposing the system under which we live today because I believe it is subversive of the best interests of the people. I am not satisfied with things as they are, and I know that no matter what administration is in power, even were it a Socialist administration, there will be no material change in the condition of the people until we have a new social system based upon the mutual economic interests of the whole people; until you and I and all of us collectively own those things that we collectively need and use.

That is a basic economic proposition. As long as a relatively few men own the railroads, the telegraph, the telephone, own the oil fields and the gas fields and the steel mills and the sugar refineries and the leather tanneries—own, in short, the sources and means of life—they will corrupt our politics, they will enslave the working class, they will impoverish and debase society, they will do all things that are needful to perpetuate their power as the economic masters and the political rulers of the people. Not until these great agencies are owned and operated by the people can the people hope for any material improvement in their social condition.

Is the condition fair today, and satisfactory to the thinking man? According to the most reliable reports at our command, as I speak here this afternoon there are at least four millions of workingmen vainly searching for employment. Have you ever found yourself in that unspeakably sad predicament? Have you ever had to go up the street, begging for work, in a great city thronged with humanity—and, by the way, my friends, people are never quite so strange to each other as when they are forced into artificial, crowded and stifled relationship.

I would rather be friendless out on the American desert than to be friendless in New York or Chicago. Have you ever walked up one side of the street and come back on the other side, while your wife, Mary, was waiting at home with three or four children for you to report that you had found work? Quite fortunately for me I had an experience of similar nature quite early in my life. Quite fortunately because, had I not known from my own experience just what it is to have to beg for work, just what it is to be shown the door as if I were a very offensive intruder, had I not known what it is to suffer for the want of food, had I not seen every door closed and barred in my face, had I not found myself friendless and alone in the city as a boy looking for work, and in vain, perhaps I would not be here this afternoon. I might have grown up as some others have who have been, as they regard themselves, fortunate. I might have waved aside my fellowmen and said, "Do as I have done. If you are without work it is your own fault. Look at me; I am self-made. No man is under the necessity of looking for work if he is willing to work."

Nothing is more humiliating than to have to beg for work, and a system in which any man has to beg for work stands condemned. No man can defend it. Now the rights of one are as sacred as the rights of a million. Suppose you happen to be the one who has no work. This republic is a failure so far as you are concerned.

Every man has the inalienable right to work.

Here I stand, just as I was created. I have two hands that represent my labor power. I have some bone and muscle and sinew and some energy. I want to exchange the use of these for food and clothing and shelter. But between me and the tools with which work is done there stands a man artificially created. He says, "No, no!" Why not? "Because you cannot first make a profit for me."

Now, there has been a revolution in industry during the last fifty years, but the trouble with most people is that they haven't kept pace with it. They don't know anything about it, and they are especially innocent in regard to it in the small western cities and states, where the same old conditions of a century ago still largely prevail. Your grandfather could help himself anywhere. All he needed was some cheap, simple primitive tools and he could then apply his labor to the resources of nature with his individual tools and produce what he needed. That era in our history produced our greatest men. Lincoln himself sprang from this primitive state of society. People have said, "Why, he had no chance. See how great he became." Yes, but Lincoln had for his comrades great, green-plumed forest monarchs. He could put his arms about them and hear their heart-throbs, as they whispered: "Go on, Abe, a great destiny awaits you." He was in partnership with nature. He associated with birds and bees and flowers, and he was in the fields and heard the rippling music of the laughing brooks and streams. Nature took him to her bosom and nourished him, and from his unpolluted heart there sprang his noble aspirations.

Had Lincoln been born in a sweatshop he would never have been heard of.

How is it with the babe that is born in Mott street, or in the lower Bowery, or in the east side of New York City? That is where thousands, tens of thousands and hundreds of thousands of babes are born who are to constitute our future generations.

I have seen children ten years of age in New York City who had never seen a live chicken. The babes there don't know what it is to put their tiny feet on a blade of grass. It is the most densely populated spot on earth.

You have seen your beehive—just fancy a human beehive of which yours is the miniature and you have the industrial hive under capitalism. If you have never seen this condition you are excusable for not being a Socialist. Come to New York, Chicago, San Francisco with me; remain with me just twenty-four hours, and then look into my face as I shall look into yours when I ask: "What about Socialism now?" These children by hundreds and thousands are born in sub-cellars, where a whole grown family is crowded together in one room, where modesty between the sexes is absolutely impossible. They are surrounded by filth and vermin. From their birth they see nothing but immorality and vice and crime. They are tainted in the cradle. They are inoculated by their surroundings and they are doomed from the beginning. This system takes their lives just as certainly as if a dagger were thrust into their quivering little hearts, and let me say to you that it were better for many thousands of them if they had never seen the light.

Now I submit, my friends, that such a condition as this is indefensible in the twentieth century. Time was when everything had to be done in a very primitive way, and most men had to work all their days, all their lives, to feed and shelter themselves. They had no time, they had no opportunity for higher development, and so they were what the world calls "illiterate." They had little chance. It took all their time and energy to feed the animal; but how is it today? Upon the average twenty men can today, with the aid of modern machinery, produce as much wealth as a thousand did a half century ago. Can you think of a single thing that enters into our daily existence that can not be easily produced in abundance for all? If you can I wish you would do me the kindness to name it.

I don't know it all. I am simply a student of this great question, and I am serving as best I can, and I know my eyes are ready for the light, and I thank that man, no matter what he be, who can add to the flame of the torch I bear. If there is a single thing that you can think of that cannot be produced in abundance, name it. Bread, clothing, fuel—everything is here.

Nature's storehouse is full to the surface of the earth. All of the raw materials are deposited here in abundance. We have the most marvelous machinery the world has ever known. Man has long since become master of the natural forces and made them work for him. Now he has but to touch a button and the wheels begin to spin and the machinery to whirr, and wealth is produced on every hand in increasing abundance.

Why should any man, woman or child suffer for food, clothing or shelter? Why? The question cannot be answered. Don't tell me that some men are too lazy to work. Suppose they are too lazy to work, what do you think of a social system that produces men too lazy to work? If a man is too lazy to work, don't treat him with contempt. Don't look down upon him with scorn as if you were a superior being. If there is a man who is too lazy to work there is something the matter with him. He wasn't born right or he was perverted in this system. You could not, if you tried, keep a normal man inactive, and if you did he would go stark mad. Go to any penitentiary and you will find the men there begging for the privilege of doing work.

I know by close study of the question exactly how men become idle. I don't repel them when I meet them. I have never yet seen the tramp I was not able to receive with open arms. He is a little less fortunate than I am. He is made the same as I am made. He is a child of the same Father. Had I been born in his environment, had I been subjected to the same things to which he was, I would have been where he is.

Can you tell me why there wasn't a tramp in the United States in 1860? In that day, if some one had said "tramp," no one would have known what was meant by it. If human nature is innately depraved and men would rather ride on brake-beams and sleep in holes and caves instead of comfortable beds, if they would do that from pure choice and from natural depravity, why were they not built that way fifty years ago? Fifty years ago capitalism was in its earlier stages. Fifty years ago work was still mainly done by hand, and every boy could learn a trade, and every boy could master the tools and go to work. That is why there were no tramps. In fifty years that simple tool has become a mammoth machine. It gets larger and larger all the time. It has crowded the hand tool out of production. With the machine came the capitalist.

There were no capitalists, nor was there such a thing as capital before the beginning of the present system. Capitalists came with machinery. Up to the time that machinery supplanted the hand tool the little employer was himself a workingman. No matter what the shop or factory, you would find the employer working side by side with his men. He was a superior workman who got more orders than he could fill and employed others to help him, but he had to pay them the equivalent of what they produced because if he did not they would pack up their tools and go into business for themselves.

Now, the individual tool has become the mammoth machine. It has multiplied production by hundreds. The old tool was individually owned and used. The modern tool, in the form of a great machine, is social in every conception of it. Look at one of these giant machines. Come to the *Appeal* office and look at the press in operation. Here the progressive conception of the ages is crystallized. What individual shall put his hand on this social agency and say, "This is mine! He who would apply labor here must first pay tribute to me."

The hand tool has been very largely supplanted by this machine. Not many tools are left. You are still producing in a very small way here in Girard, but your production is flickering out gradually. It is but a question of time until it will expire entirely. In spite of all that can be said or done to the contrary, production is organizing upon a larger and larger scale and becoming entirely co-operative. This has crowded out the smaller competitor and gradually opened the way for a new social order.

Your material interest and mine in the society of the future will be the same. Instead of having to fight each other like animals, as we do today, and seeking to glorify the brute struggle for existence—of which every civilized human being ought to be ashamed—instead of this, our material interests are going to be mutual. We are going to jointly own these mammoth machines, and we are going to operate them as joint partners, and we are going to divide all the products among ourselves.

We are not going to send our surplus to the Goulds and Vanderbilts of New York. We are not going to pile up a billion of dollars in John D. Rockefeller's hands—a vast pyramid from the height of which he can look down with scorn and contempt upon the "common herd." John D. Rockefeller's great fortune is built upon your ignorance. When you know enough to know what your interest is you will support the great party that is organized upon the principle of collective ownership of the means of life. This party will sweep into power upon the issue of emancipation, just as republicanism swept into power upon the abolition question half a century ago.

In the meantime, don't have any fear of us Socialists. We don't mean any harm! Many of you have been taught to look upon us as very dangerous people. It is amazing to what extent this prejudice has struck root. The capitalist press will tell you of a good many evil things that we Socialists are going to do that we never intend to do. They will tell you we are going to break up the home. Great heaven! What about the homes of the four million tramps that are looking for work today? How about the thousands and thousands of miserable shacks in New York and every great city where humanity festers? It would be a good thing if they were torn down and obliterated completely, for they are not fit for human habitation. No, we are not going to destroy the home, but we are going to make the home possible for the first time in history.

You may think you are very comfortable. Let me make you a little comparison. You may not agree with me. I don't expect you to and I don't ask you to. I am going to ask you to remember what I say this afternoon and perhaps before I am elected president of the United States you will believe what I say is true. Now there are those of you who are fairly comfortable under the present standard. Isn't it amazing to you how little the average man is satisfied with? You go out here to the edge of town and you find a small farmer who has a cabin with just room enough to keep himself and wife and two or three children, which has a mortgage on it, and he works early and late and gets just enough in net returns to keep him in working order, and he will deliver a lecture about the wonderful prosperity of the country.

He is satisfied, and that is his calamity.

Now, the majority of you would say that is his good fortune. "It is a blessing that he is satisfied." I want to see if I can show you that it is a curse to him and to society that he is satisfied.

If it had not been for the discontent of a few fellows who have not been satisfied with their condition you would still be living in caves. You never would have emerged from the jungle. Intelligent discontent is the mainspring of civilization.

Progress is born of agitation. It is agitation or stagnation. I have taken my choice.

This farmer works all day long, works hard enough to produce enough to live the life of a man; not of an animal, but of a man. Now there is an essential difference between a man and an animal. I admire a magnificent animal in any form except in the human form. Suppose you had everything that you could possibly desire, so far as your physical wants are concerned. Suppose you had a million to your credit in the bank, a palatial home and relations to suit yourself, but no soul capacity for real enjoyment. If you were denied knowing what sorrow is, what real joy is, what music is, and literature and sculpture, and all of those subtle influences that touch the heart and quicken the pulses and fire the senses, and so lift and ennoble a man that he can feel his head among the stars and in communion with God himself—if you are denied these, no matter how sleek or fat or contented you may be, you are still as base and as corrupt and as repulsive a being as walks God's green earth.

You may have plenty of money. The poorest people on this earth are those who have most money. A man is said to be poor who has none, but he is a pauper who has nothing else. Now this farmer, what does he know about literature? After his hard day's work is done, here he sits in his little shack. He is fed, and his animal wants are satisfied. It is at this time that a man begins to live. It is not while you work and slave that you live. It is when you have done your work honestly, when you have contributed your share to the common fund, that you begin to live. Then, as Whitman said, you can take out your soul; you can commune with yourself; you can take a comrade by the hand and you can look into his eyes and down into his soul, and in that holy communion you live. And if you don't know what that is, or if you are not at least on the edge of it, it is denied you to even look into the promised land.

Now this farmer knows nothing about the literature of the world. All its libraries are sealed to him. So far as he is concerned, Homer and Dante and Dickens might as well not have lived; Beethoven, Liszt and Wagner, and all those musicians whose art makes the common atmosphere blossom with harmony, never have been for this farmer. He knows nothing about poetry or art. Never rises above the animal plane upon which he is living. Within fifteen minutes after he has ceased to live he is forgotten; the next generation doesn't know his name, and the world doesn't know he ever lived. That is life under the present standard.

You tell me that is all the farmer is fit for? What do I propose to do for that farmer? Nothing. I only want him to know that he is robbed every day in the week, and if I can awaken him to the fact that he is robbed under the capitalist system he will fall into line with the Socialist movement, and will march to the polls on election day, and instead of casting his vote to fasten the shackles upon his limbs more firmly, he will vote for his emancipation. All I have to do is to show that farmer, that day laborer, that tramp, that they are victims of this system, that their interests are identical, that they constitute the millions and that the millions have the votes. The Rockefellers have the dollars, but we have the votes; and when we have sense enough to know how to use the votes we will have not only the votes but the dollars for all the children of men.

This seems quite visionary to some of you, and especially to those of you who know nothing about economics. I could not begin to tell you the story of social evolution this afternoon; of how these things are doing day by day, of how the world is being pushed into Socialism, and how it is bound to arrive, no matter whether you are for it or against it. It is the next inevitable phase of civilization. It isn't a scheme, it isn't a contrivance. It isn't anything that is made to order. The day is coming when you will be pushed into it by unseen hands whether you will or not. Nothing can be introduced until the people want it, and when the majority want it they will know how to get it.

I venture the prophecy that within the next five years you will be completely dispossessed. You are howling against the trusts, and the trusts are laughing at you. You keep on voting in the same old way, and the trusts keep on getting what you produce. You say Congress will give you some relief. Good heavens! Who will save us from Congress? Don't you know that Congress is made up almost wholly of trust lawyers and corporation attorneys? I don't happen to have the roll of this one, but with few exceptions they are all lawyers. Now, in the competitive system the lawyer sells himself to the highest bidder the same as the workingman does. Who is the highest bidder? The trust and corporation, of course. So the trust buys the best lawyer and the common herd gets the shyster.

Now it is a fact that politics is simply the reflex of economics. The material foundation of society determines the character of all social institutions—political, educational, ethical and spiritual. In exact proportion as the economic foundation of society changes the character of all social institutions changes to correspond to that basis. Half of this country was in favor of chattel slavery, and half was opposed to it, geographically speaking. Why was the church of the South in favor of chattel slavery? Why was the church of the North opposed to chattel slavery? The northern capitalist wasn't a bit more opposed to chattel slavery from any moral sense than was the southern plantation owner. The South produced cotton for the market by the hand labor of negro slaves. On the other hand, the North wasn't dependent upon cotton— could raise no cotton. In the North it was the small capitalist at the beginning of capitalism, who, with the machine, had begun to manufacture, and wanted cheap labor; and the sharper the competition the cheaper he could buy his labor. Now, chattel slavery to the southern plantation owner was the source of his wealth. He had to have slaves, and what the plantation owner had to have in economics the preacher had to justify in religion. As long as chattel slavery was necessary to the southern plantation owner, as long as that stage of the economic condition lasted, the preachers stood up in the pulpits of the South and said it was ordained of God, and proved it by the Bible. I don't know of any crime that the oppressors and their hirelings have not proven by the Bible.

Then competition between workers began as machines took the place of hand labor. Manufacturers wanted larger and larger bodies of labor and that competition spread out here to Kansas, and I have always felt when in Kansas that I stood on sacred soil. When I hear the name of Kansas I doff my hat in reverence. The free soilers came here, despised, hated and persecuted. They were the enemies of the human race. Why? Because they had hearts throbbing within their breasts. Because they looked with compassion upon the negro slave who received his wages in lashes applied to his naked back; who saw his crying wife torn from him and his children, pleading, snatched from his side and sold into slavery, while the great mass looked on just as the great mass is looking on today, and the preachers stood up in their pulpits and said: "It is all right. It is God-ordained." And whenever an abolitionist raised his head he was persecuted and hounded as if he had been a wild beast.

I heard this story from Wendell Phillips one evening. I never can forget it. How I wish he were here this afternoon! We sat together and he said: "Debs, the world will never know with what bitter and relentless persecution the early abolitionists had to contend."

Wendell Phillips was the most perfect aristocrat in the true sense I have ever seen; came nearest being a perfect man. And yet he was treated as if he had been the worst felon on earth. They went to his house one night to mob him, and why? Because he protested against sending a young negro girl back into slavery. They came to take her back, and the whole commonwealth of Massachusetts said, "Take her back! Obey the law!" That is what they are everlastingly saying to us—"Obey the law!" Just above the door of the state house there was an inscription: "God bless the Common-wealth of Massachusetts." Wendell Phillips said: "If Massachusetts has become a slave hunter, if Massachusetts is in alliance with the slave catchers of the south, the inscription over that portal should be changed, and in place of 'God Bless the Common-wealth of Massachusetts' it should be: 'God Damn the Com-monwealth of Massachusetts!' " God smiled in that same instant.

All of the slave catchers and holders, all of the oppressors of man, all of the enemies of the human race, all of the rulers of Siberia, where a large part of this earth's surface has been trans-formed into a hell—all have spoken in the name of the Great God and in the name of the Holy Bible.

There will be a change one of these days. The world is just beginning to awaken, and is soon to sing its first anthem of free-dom. All the signs of the times are cheering. Twenty-five years ago there was but a handful of Socialists; today there are a half million. When the polls are closed next fall you will be astounded. The Socialist movement is in alliance with the forces of progress. We are today where the abolitionists were in 1858. They had a million and a quarter of votes. There was dissension in the Whig, Republican and Free Soil parties, but the time had come for a great change, and the Republican party was formed in spite of the bickerings and contentions of men. Lincoln made the great speech in that year that gave him the nomination and afterward made him President of the United States.

If you had said to the people in 1858, "In two years from now the Republican party is going to sweep the country and seat the President," you would have been laughed to scorn. The Socialist party stands today where the Republican party stood fifty years ago. It is in alliance with the forces of evolution, the one party that has a clear-cut, overmastering, overshadowing issue; the party that stands for the people, and the only party that stands for all the people. In this system we have one set who are called capitalists, and another set who are called workers; and they are at war with each other.

Now, we Socialists propose that society in its collective capacity shall produce, not for profit, but in abundance to satisfy human wants; that every man shall have the inalienable right to work, and receive the full equivalent of all he produces; that every man may stand fearlessly erect in the pride and majesty of his own manhood.

Every man and every woman will then be economically free. They can, without let or hindrance, apply their labor, with the best machinery that can be devised, to all the natural resources, do the work of society and produce for all; and then receive in exchange a certificate of value equivalent to that of their production. Then society will improve its institutions in proportion to the progress of invention. Whether in the city or on the farm, all things productive will be carried forward on a gigantic scale. All industry will be completely organized. Society for the first time will have a scientific foundation. Every man, by being economically free, will have some time for himself. He can then take a full and perfect breath. He can enjoy life with his wife and children, because then he will have a home.

We are not going to destroy private property. We are going to establish private property—all the private property necessary to house man, keep him in comfort and satisfy his wants. Eighty per cent of the people of the United States have no property today. A few have got it all. They have dispossessed the people, and when we get into power we will dispossess them. We will reduce the workday and give every man a chance. We will go to the parks, and we will have music, because we will have time to play music and desire to hear it.

Is it not sad to think that not one in a thousand knows what music is? Is it not pitiable to see the poor, ignorant, dumb human utterly impervious to the divine influences of music? If humanity could only respond to the higher influences! And it would if it had time.

Release the animal, throw off his burden; give him a chance and he rises as if by magic to the plane of a man. Man has all of the divine attributes. They are in a latent state. They are not yet developed. It does not pay now to love music. Keep your eye on the almighty dollar and your fellowman. Get the dollar and keep him down. Make him produce for you. You are not your brother's keeper. Suppose he is poor! Suppose his wife is forced into prostitution! Suppose his child is deformed! And suppose he shuffles off by destroying himself! What is that to you?

But you ought to be ashamed. Take the standard home and look it in the face. If you know what that standard means, and you are a success, God help the failure!

Our conduct is determined by our economic relations. If you and I must fight each other to exist, we will not love each other very hard. We can go to the same church and hear the same minister tell us in good conscience that we ought to love each other, and the next day we approach some business transaction. Do we remember what the minister told us? No; it is gone until next Sunday. Six days in the week we are following the Golden Rule reversed. Now, when we approach a business transaction in competition, what is more natural than that we should try to get the better of it?—get the better of our fellow man?—cheat him if we can?

And if you succeed, that fixes you as a business man. You have all the necessary qualifications. Don't let your conscience disturb you—that would interfere with business.

Competition was natural enough at one time, but do you think you are competing today? Many of you think you are competing. Against whom? Against Rockefeller? About as I would if I had a wheelbarrow and competed with the Santa Fe from here to Kansas City. That is about the way you are competing; but your boys will not have even that chance—if capitalism lives that long. You hear of the "late" panic. It is very late. It is going to be very late. This panic will be with us five years from now, and will continue till then.

I am not a prophet. I can no more penetrate the future than you can. I do study the forces that underlie society and the trend of evolution. I can tell by what we have passed through about what we will have in the future; and I know that capitalism can be abolished and the people put in possession. Now, when we have taken possession, and we jointly own the means of production, we will no longer have to fight each other to live; our interests, instead of being competitive, will be co-operative. We will work side by side. Your interest will be mine and mine will be yours. That is the economic condition from which will spring the humane social relation of the future.

When we are in partnership and have stopped clutching each other's throats, when we have stopped enslaving each other, we will stand together, hands clasped, and be friends. We will be comrades, we will be brothers, and we will begin the march to the grandest civilization the human race have ever known.

I did not mean to keep you so long this afternoon. I am sure I appreciate the patience with which you have listened to me. From the very depths of my heart I thank you, each of you—every man, woman and child—for this splendid testimonial, this beautiful tribute, which I shall remember with gratitude and love until memory empties its urn into forgetfulness.

Unionism versus Socialism

SAMUEL GOMPERS

Samuel Gompers was born in London in 1850. The son of a Jewish cigarmaker, Gompers himself was apprenticed in that craft. The family migrated to New York City in 1863, and the next year Gompers joined the Cigarmakers' Union, becoming president of Local 144. The national president of the union, Adolph Strasser, promoted Gompers' fortunes, and when in 1886 a federation of national unions took the name American Federation of Labor, Gompers was elected president. He held that office until his death in 1924, with the exception of one term. The chief opposition to his emphasis on immediate gains in wages, hours, and working conditions came from the strong Socialist minority in the labor movement, which in 1902 set up the American Labor Union as a rival federation of class-conscious unions aiming at the destruction of capitalism. Alarmed by this threat of dual unionism, Gompers attacked the Socialist resolutions introduced into the AFL national convention in 1903. Here is most of his speech, after which the resolutions were defeated by a six-to-one majority, from *Report of Proceedings of the 23rd National Convention of the American Federation of Labor* (1903).

MR. CHAIRMAN and fellow delegates, I am always impressed with an earnest man's utterances, and to me a man who makes a statement and gives me an assurance, my disposition has always been to be credulous and to believe him. When an organization makes a declaration, my disposition is to believe it. I am always inclined to believe a man or an aggregation of men to be honest, but when I discover that a man has made professions of one thing and his actions belie his words, then I am like the Missourian; after that, so far as he is concerned, he must show me.

Vice-President Duncan has not the opportunity to reply to his critics, because of his calling attention to the conduct of the men who clothed themselves in the mantle of Socialism, and assumed a position of superiority, mentally, in honesty, in work, and in ennobling purposes. It is because their professions are in entire discord with their actions in this Convention that it is necessary to call their position in question.

I shall not refer at this time to their very many detailed acts of treachery to the trade-union movement; but I shall refer to some of the declarations made upon the floor of this Convention by delegates participating in this discussion, and show you that though they may believe themselves to be trade-unionists, they are at heart, and logically, the antagonists of our movement.

I want to say, and I am sure it will come as a shock to the brother, for between Mr. Hayes and myself—I mean Max Hayes —personally there has, I think, existed a very close and sympathetic bond of friendship, but here we differ—I am a trade-unionist; he thinks he is.

Delegate Hayes, I firmly believe, was ill when he came to this Convention. He could not accept a duty which was meant as a compliment, and has been so regarded by other men, to perform committee work; but if ever a man made an effort and showed that he was sacrificing his vitality, he did in making his address upon a speculative theory which, undoubtedly, he thought more important than the doing of the essential work of the Convention.

Our friends, the Socialists, always when with us have an excellent conception of the trouble in our industrial life. They say, as we say, and as every intelligent man or woman says, that there are miseries which surround us. We recognize the poverty, we know the sweatshop, we can play on every string of the harp, and touch the tenderest chords of human sympathy; but while we recognize the evil and would apply the remedy, our Socialist friends would look forward to the promised land, and wait for "the sweet by-and-by." Their statements as to economic ills are right; their conclusions and their philosophy are all askew.

The action of the committee has been found fault with because they did not bring in a substitute for the resolutions presented, but instead took a course that will bring this matter fairly and squarely before the Convention. At the last Convention in New Orleans, through placing us in a false position, the resolution upon this question came within an ace of being adopted; but this year the committee has made this question a plain, broad proposition.

The vote that will be recorded here today against the report of the committee will be fairly and squarely recorded in favor of Socialism; and the vote that is recorded in favor of the committee's report will be against Socialism. And it will be recognized as such throughout the land.

There has not been a legislative body before which the other officers of the Federation or I myself have appeared, nor an association of employers, nor individual employers with whom we have met in conference but that we have been confronted with this Socialistic amendment, so-called, which came near being passed at New Orleans. It has made, and will make, our work doubly difficult, because these employers have refused and do refuse to confer for the adjustment of difficulties and disputes when they are led to believe by declaration that property is in danger of confiscation.

We have been asked how many trade-unionists there are in Congress. I venture to say that there are more trade-unionists in Congress and in our state Legislatures holding clear cards than there are elsewhere in similar positions the world over. Do you suppose the Socialists want trade-unionists elected to Congress and to the Legislatures?

[Delegate J. Keyes: "No."]

Of course, no. Of course, Socialist Brother Keyes, no. I am proud of you, Brother Keyes, for your honesty in admitting it. But what Brother Keyes has just admitted on the floor is true of every other Socialist in the Convention. As a matter of fact, wherever there has been a trade-unionist candidate for any political office, if there have been half a dozen Socialists in town, they have always tried to defeat the trade-unionists.

Now, there has been a remark made about the passage of the military law by Congress. I agree it would have been a good thing if we could have prevented the passage of that law, but the delegate said that if we even had a minority in Congress, it could not have become law. I point him to the fact that in Germany they have the largest number of any party in the parliament of that country, and yet they have the most tyrannical military laws of any country on the globe.

It is all very well to make a declaration, but the facts are another thing. We are told we ought not to rely upon an indiscreet remark by a Socialist here and there; but if not, then why rely upon the remarks of trade-unionists here and there? Yes, an indiscreet remark—but the difficulty here and outside of the Conventions of the American Federation of Labor is to find a Socialist who is not all the time guilty of making indiscreet remarks. He is at it all the time. . . .

For that reason I am not with those parties, and one of the reasons I am not with your party is because I want to be in line with the declaration that the trade-union policy, the movement and the work must be unhampered by your political nostrums.

When the Socialists formed the American Labor Union in rivalry to the American Federation of Labor, I took occasion to continually say in the American Federationist that it was but another attempt to form another Socialist Trade and Labor Alliance, without its practical courage to openly declare its enmity to the American trade-union movement.

Is it not a fact that no matter what we achieve, we are belittled by the Socialists? Even the Labor Day we have achieved for all the people of our country—the proposition comes in here to abolish it and to make Labor Day in line with the Labor Day of continental Europe, May 1st. The American Federation of Labor in 1879 addressed a letter to the French workingmen, suggesting to them to celebrate the 1st of May when the carpenters were to inaugurate the eight-hour day; and from that suggestion, made by your humble servant, they have made the first of May of each year their holiday, and so they celebrate it, usually on the Sunday before or the Sunday after. They take no holiday, but they sometimes celebrate it in the evening of May 1st.

In no country on the globe has labor ever taken a day for itself without asking consent, or begging or apologizing for itself, except in this country. And yet the Socialists want us to give up our own Labor Day and celebrate on May 1st, in the evening.

The secretary of the Socialist party has severed his connection with the reformed (?) Socialist party, because of his being opposed to the hostile tactics of that party to the trade-unions; and, being at heart a trade-unionist, he was forced out of his position. Since that time he has given to the world the real reasons why he was forced out—because he dared to stand up in defense of trades-unions and against the policy of antagonizing the trades-unions and hoisting up the American Labor Union.

Is it not true, to a very great extent, that your Socialist American Labor Union, except the miners and a very few others, is made up very largely of expelled members of the trades-unions who broke faith with their fellow-workmen? Do you Socialists here deny it? Your official papers say so, and your Socialist organizers' reports admit it. Are your unions not boycotting the International Boot and Shoe Workers' Union label and the International Paper Makers' Union label, and other international unions, and where they do not boycott them, hold the threat over the heads of some other unions, compelling them either to submit, or forcing them to waver in their fealty and loyalty to the movement?

The cigar-makers' union of Denver has had this condition of things confront it. They were threatened with a Socialist boycott of their label, and their president and those poor fellows, many of whom can not labor elsewhere, must submit to the dictates of the Socialist organization, for they have no other alternative except to get out of Denver. Because they can not otherwise work and support themselves, they must submit, or be boycotted by Socialists out of the beneficent climate of Denver, and driven elsewhere, to pine away from the ravages of that dread disease from which so many suffer and by reason of which they sought that climate for the relief afforded.

Men of labor, if you were in the office of the American Federation of Labor for a time and you knew the things that transpire in the labor movement in a general and in a specific way—for they are all focussed there, and we know what is going on and we know the enemies of the labor movement—you would have your opinion clear cut upon this subject. Why, we have spent more money in organizing in Colorado itself than in any other state, notwithstanding that, industrially considered, it ought to cost very little.

I want to tell you, Socialists, that I have studied your philosophy; read your works upon economics, and not the meanest of them;

studied your standard works, both in English and German—have
not only read, but studied them. I have heard your orators and
watched the work of your movement the world over. I have kept
close watch upon your doctrines for thirty years; have been closely
associated with many of you, and know how you think and what
you propose. I know, too, what you have up your sleeve. And I
want to say that I am entirely at variance with your philosophy. I
declare it to you, I am not only at variance with your doctrines, but
with your philosophy. Economically, you are unsound; socially,
you are wrong; industrially, you are an impossibility.

A Modern Lear

JANE ADDAMS

Jane Addams (1860–1935) and her associates at Hull-House in Chicago were probably the most remarkable group of women ever to assemble in the United States. Miss Addams acquired much of her idealism and also her ability at practical politics from her father, a Quaker who served eight terms in the state senate of Illinois from the village of Cedarville. After attending Rockford Seminary in Illinois and consuming some years on physical and emotional distress, she went on a tour of Europe with a Rockford classmate. In London they saw the world's first settlement house, Toynbee Hall, and conceived the notion of a similar institution in the United States. Hull-House, the focal point of Jane Addams' activities for the rest of her life, opened in 1890. Four years later Miss Addams was a member of a committee from the Chicago Civic Federation which tried vainly to persuade the Pullman company to arbitrate the strike of 1894. The attitudes and processes that gave rise to that cataclysmic event led Jane Addams to philosophize about leadership in a democracy; her analysis was published in *Satellite Cities,* edited by Graham Taylor (New York: D. Appleton, 1915), reprinted from *Survey* for November 2, 1912.

THOSE OF US who lived in Chicago during the summer of 1894 were confronted by a drama which epitomized and, at the same time, challenged the code of social ethics under which we live, for a quick series of unusual events had dispelled the good nature which in happier times envelops the ugliness of the industrial situation. It sometimes seems as if the shocking experiences of that summer, the barbaric instinct to kill, roused on both sides, the sharp division into class lines, with the resultant distrust and bitterness, can only be endured if we learn from it all a great ethical lesson. To endure is all we can hope for. It is impossible to justify such a course of rage and riot in a civilized community to whom the methods of conciliation and control were open. Every public-spirited citizen in Chicago during that summer felt the stress and perplexity of the situation and asked himself, "How far am I responsible for this social disorder? What can be done to prevent such outrageous manifestations of ill-will?"

If the responsibility of tolerance lies with those of the widest vision, it behooves us to consider this great social disaster, not alone in its legal aspect nor in its sociological bearings, but from those deep human motives, which, after all, determine events.

During the discussions which followed the Pullman strike, the defenders of the situation were broadly divided between the people pleading for individual benevolence and those insisting upon social righteousness; between those who held that the philanthropy of the president of the Pullman Company had been most ungratefully received and those who maintained that the situation was the inevitable outcome of the social consciousness developing among working people.

In the midst of these discussions the writer found her mind dwelling upon a comparison which modified and softened all her judgments. Her attention was caught by the similarity of ingratitude suffered by an indulgent employer and an indulgent parent. *King Lear* came often to her mind. We have all shared the family relationship and our code of ethics concerning it is somewhat settled. We also bear a part in the industrial relationship, but our ethics concerning that are still uncertain. A comparative study of these two relationships presents an advantage, in that it enables us to consider the situation from the known experience toward the unknown. The minds of all of us reach back to our early struggles, as we emerged from the state of self-willed childhood to a recognition of the family claim.

We have all had glimpses of what it might be to blaspheme against family ties, to ignore the elemental claim they make upon us; but on the whole we have recognized them, and it does not occur to us to throw them over. The industrial claim is so difficult; the ties are so intangible that we are constantly ignoring them and shirking the duties which they impose. It will probably be easier to treat of the tragedy of the Pullman strike as if it were already long past when we compare it to the family tragedy of Lear, which has already become historic to our minds and which we discuss without personal feeling.

Historically considered, the relation of Lear to his children was archaic and barbaric, holding in it merely the beginnings of a family life, since developed. We may in later years learn to look back upon the industrial relationships in which we are now placed as quite as incomprehensible and selfish, quite as barbaric and undeveloped, as was the family relationship between Lear and his daughters. We may then take the relationship of this unusually generous employer at Pullman to his own townful of employees as at least a fair one, because so exceptionally liberal in many of its aspects. King Lear doubtless held the same notion of a father's duty that was held by the other fathers of his time; but he alone was a king and had kingdoms to bestow upon his children. He was unique, therefore, in the magnitude of his indulgence, and in the magnitude of the disaster which followed it. The sense of duty held by the president of the Pullman Company doubtless represents the ideal in the minds of the best of the present employers as to their obligations toward their employees, but he projected this ideal more magnificently than the others. He alone gave his men so model a town, such perfect surroundings. The magnitude of his indulgence and failure corresponded, and we are forced to challenge the ideal itself: the same ideal which, more or less clearly defined, is floating in the minds of all philanthropic employers.

This older tragedy implied maladjustment between individuals; the forces of the tragedy were personal and passionate. This modern tragedy in its inception is a maladjustment between two large bodies of men: an employing company and a mass of employees. It deals not with personal relationship, but with industrial relationships.

Owing, however, to the unusual part played in it by the will of one man, we find that it closely approaches *Lear* in motif. The relation of the British King to his family is very like the relation of the president of the Pullman Company to his town; the dénouement of a daughter's break with her father suggests the break of the employees with their benefactor. If we call one an example of the domestic tragedy, the other of the industrial tragedy, it is possible to make them illuminate each other.

It is easy to discover striking points of similarity in the tragedies of the royal father and the philanthropic president of the Pullman Company. The like quality of ingratitude they both suffered is at once apparent. It may be said that the ingratitude which Lear received was poignant and bitter to him in proportion as he recalled the extraordinary benefits he had heaped upon his daughters, and that he found his fate harder to bear because he had so far exceeded the measure of a father's duty, as he himself says. What, then, would be the bitterness of a man who had heaped extraordinary benefits upon those toward whom he had no duty recognized by common consent; who had not only exceeded the righteousness of the employer, but who had worked out original and striking methods for lavishing goodness and generosity? More than that, the president had been almost persecuted for this goodness by the more utilitarian members of his company and had at one time imperiled his business reputation for the sake of the benefactions to his town, and he had thus reached the height of sacrifice for it. This model town embodied not only his hopes and ambitions, but stood for the peculiar effort which a man makes for that which is misunderstood.

It is easy to see that although the heart of Lear was cut by ingratitude and by misfortune, it was cut deepest of all by the public pity of his people, in that they should remember him no longer as a king and benefactor, but as a defeated man who had blundered through oversoftness. So the heart of the Chicago man was cut by the unparalleled publicity which brought him to the minds of thousands as a type of oppression and injustice, and to many others as an example of the evil of an irregulated sympathy for the "lower classes." He who had been dined and fêted throughout Europe as the creator of a model town, as the friend and benefactor of workingmen, was now execrated by workingmen throughout the entire country. He had not only been good to those who were now basely ungrateful to him, but he felt himself deserted by the admiration of his people.

In shops such as those at Pullman, indeed, in all manufacturing affairs since the industrial revolution, industry is organized into a vast social operation. The shops are managed, however, not for the development of the workman thus socialized, but for the interests of the company owning the capital. The divergence between the social form and the individual aim becomes greater as the employees are more highly socialized and dependent, just as the clash in a family is more vital in proportion to the development and closeness of the family tie. The president of the Pullman Company went further than the usual employer does. He socialized not only the factory but the form in which his workmen were living. He built and, in a great measure, regulated an entire town. This again might have worked out into a successful associated effort if he had had in view the sole good of the inhabitants thus socialized, if he had called upon them for self-expression and had made the town a growth and manifestation of their wants and needs. But, unfortunately, the end to be obtained became ultimately commercial and not social, having in view the payment to the company of at least 4 per cent. on the money invested, so that with this rigid requirement there could be no adaptation of rent to wages, much less to needs. The rents became statical and the wages competitive, shifting inevitably with the demands of trade. The president assumed that he himself knew the needs of his men, and so far from wishing them to express their needs he denied to them the simple rights of trade organization, which would have been, of course, the merest preliminary to an attempt at associated expression. If we may take the dictatorial relation of Lear to Cordelia as a typical and most dramatic example of the distinctively family tragedy, one will asserting its authority through all the entanglement of wounded affection, and insisting upon its selfish ends at all costs, may we not consider the absolute authority of this employer over his town as a typical and dramatic example of the industrial tragedy? One will directing the energies of many others, without regard to their desires, and having in view in the last analysis only commercial results?

It shocks our ideal of family life that a man should fail to know his daughter's heart because she awkwardly expressed her love, that he should refuse to comfort and advise her through all difference of opinion and clashing of will. That a man should be so absorbed in his own indignation as to fail to apprehend his child's thought; that he should lose his affection in his anger is really no more unnatural than that the man who spent a million of dollars on a swamp to make it sanitary for his employees, should refuse to speak to them for ten minutes, whether they were in the right or wrong; or that a man who had given them his time and thought for twenty years should withdraw from them his guidance when he believed them misled by ill-advisers and wandering in a mental fog; or that he should grow hard and angry when they needed tenderness and help.

Lear ignored the common ancestry of Cordelia and himself. He forgot her royal inheritance of magnanimity, and also the power of obstinacy which he shared with her. So long had he thought of himself as the noble and indulgent father that he had lost the faculty by which he might perceive himself in the wrong. Even when his spirit was broken by the storm he declared himself more sinned against than sinning. He could believe any amount of kindness and goodness of himself, but could imagine no fidelity on the part of Cordelia unless she gave him the sign he demanded.

The president of the Pullman Company doubtless began to build his town from an honest desire to give his employees the best surroundings. As it developed it became a source of pride and an exponent of power, that he cared most for when it gave him a glow of benevolence. Gradually, what the outside world thought of it became of importance to him and he ceased to measure its usefulness by the standard of the men's needs. The theater was complete in equipment and beautiful in design, but too costly for a troupe who depended upon the patronage of mechanics, as the church was too expensive to be rented continuously. We can imagine the founder of the town slowly darkening his glints of memory and forgetting the common stock of experience which he held with his men. He cultivated the great and noble impulses of the benefactor until the power of attaining a simple human relationship with his employees, that of frank equality with them, was gone from him. He, too, lost the faculty of affectionate interpretation, and demanded a sign. He and his employees had no mutual interest in a common cause.

Was not the grotesque situation of the royal father and the philanthropic employer to perform so many good deeds that they lost the power of recognizing good in beneficiaries? Were not both so absorbed in carrying out a personal plan of improvement that they failed to catch the great moral lesson which their times offered them? This is the crucial point of the tragedies and may be further elucidated.

Lear had doubtless swung a bauble before Cordelia's baby eyes that he might have the pleasure of seeing the little pink and tender hands stretched for it. A few years later, he had given jewels to the young princess, and felt an exquisite pleasure when she stood before him, delighted with her gaud and grateful to her father. He demanded the same kind of response for his gift of the kingdom, but the gratitude must be larger and more carefully expressed, as befitted such a gift. At the opening of the drama he sat upon his throne ready for this enjoyment, but instead of delight and grati-tude he found the first dawn of character. His daughter made the awkward attempt of an untrained soul to be honest, to be scrupu-lous in the expressions of its feelings. It was new to him that his child should be moved by a principle outside of himself, which even his imagination could not follow; that she had caught the no-tion of an existence so vast that her relationship as a daughter was but part of it.

Perhaps her suitors, the King of France or the Duke of Bur-gundy, had first hinted to the young Cordelia that there was a fuller life beyond the seas. Certain it is that someone had shaken her from the quiet measure of her insular existence and that she had at last felt the thrill of the world's life. She was transformed by a dignity which recast her speech and made it self-contained, as is becoming a citizen of the world. She found herself in the sweep of a notion of justice so large that the immediate loss of a kingdom seemed of little consequence to her. Even an act which might be construed as disrespect to her father was justified in her eyes be-cause she was vainly striving to fill out this large conception of duty.

The test which comes sooner or later to many parents had come to Lear, to maintain the tenderness of the relation between father and child after that relation had become one between adults; to be contented with the responses which this adult made to the family claim while, at the same time, she felt the tug upon her emotions and faculties of the larger life, the life which surrounds and completes the individual and family life, and which shares and widens her attention. He was not sufficiently wise to see that only that child can fulfill the family claim in its sweetness and strength who also fulfills the larger claim, that the adjustment of the lesser and larger implies no conflict. The mind of Lear was not big enough for this test. He failed to see anything but the personal slight involved; the ingratitude alone reached him. It was impossible for him to calmly watch his child developing beyond the strength of his own mind and sympathy.

Without pressing the analogy too hard, may we not compare the indulgent relation of this employer to his town to the relation which existed between Lear and Cordelia? He fostered his employees for many years, gave them sanitary houses and beautiful parks, but in their extreme need, when they were struggling with the most difficult question which the times could present to them, when, if ever, they required the assistance of a trained mind and a comprehensive outlook, he lost his touch and had nothing wherewith to help them. He did not see the situation. He had been ignorant of their gropings toward justice. His conception of goodness for them had been cleanliness, decency of living, and above all, thrift and temperance. He had provided them means for all this; had gone further, and given them opportunities for enjoyment and comradeship. But he suddenly found his town in the sweep of a world-wide moral impulse. A movement had been going on about him and through the souls of his workingmen of which he had been unconscious. He had only heard of this movement by rumor. The men who consorted with him at his club and in his business had spoken but little of it, and when they had discussed it had contemptuously called it the "Labor Movement," headed by deadbeats and agitators. Of the force and power of this movement, of all the vitality within it, of that conception of duty which induces men to go without food and to see their wives and children suffer for the sake of securing better wages for fellow-workmen whom they have never seen, this president had dreamed absolutely nothing. But his town had at last become swept into this large movement, so that the giving up of comfortable homes, of beautiful surroundings, seemed as naught to the men within its grasp.

Outside the ken of this philanthropist, the proletariat had learned to say in many languages that "the injury of one is the concern of all." Their watchwords were brotherhood, sacrifice, the subordination of individual and trade interests to the good of the working class; and their persistent strivings were toward the ultimate freedom of that class from the conditions under which they now labor.

Compared to these watchwords the old ones which the philanthropic employer had given his town were negative and inadequate.

When this movement finally swept in his own town, or, to speak more fairly, when in their distress and perplexity his own employees appealed to the organized manifestation of this movement, they were quite sure that simply because they were workmen in distress they would not be deserted by it. This loyalty on the part of a widely ramified and well-organized union toward the workmen in a "scab shop," who had contributed nothing to its cause, was certainly a manifestation of moral power.

That the movement was ill-directed, that it was ill-timed and disastrous in results, that it stirred up and became confused in the minds of the public with the elements of riot and bloodshed, can never touch the fact that it started from an unselfish impulse.

In none of his utterances or correspondence did the president of the company for an instant recognize this touch of nobility, although one would imagine that he would gladly point out this bit of virtue, in what he must have considered the moral ruin about him. He stood throughout pleading for the individual virtues, those which had distinguished the model workman of his youth, those which had enabled him and so many of his contemporaries to rise in life, when "rising in life" was urged upon every promising boy as the goal of his efforts. Of the new code of ethics he had caught absolutely nothing. The morals he had taught his men did not fail them in their hour of confusion. They were self-controlled and destroyed no property.[1] They were sober and exhibited no drunkenness, even though obliged to hold their meetings in the saloon hall of a neighboring town. They repaid their employer in kind,

---

[1] The bill presented to the city of Chicago by the Pullman Company for damages received during the strike was $26—the result only of petty accidents.

but he had given them no rule for the higher fellowship and life of association into which they were plunged.

The virtues of one generation are not sufficient for the next, any more than the accumulations of knowledge possessed by one age are adequate to the needs of another.

Of the virtues received from our fathers we can afford to lose none. We accept as a precious trust those principles and precepts which the race has worked out for its highest safeguard and protection. But merely to preserve those is not enough. A task is laid upon each generation to enlarge their application, to ennoble their conception, and, above all, to apply and adapt them to the peculiar problems presented to it for solution.

The president of this company desired that his employees should possess the individual and family virtues, but did nothing to cherish in them those social virtues which his own age demanded. He rather substituted for that sense of responsibility to the community, a feeling of gratitude to himself, who had provided them with public buildings, and had laid out for them a simulacrum of public life.

Is it strange that when the genuine feeling of the age struck his town this belated and almost feudal virtue of personal gratitude fell before it?

Day after day during that horrible suspense, when the wires constantly reported the same message, "The president of the company holds that there is nothing to arbitrate," one longed to find out what was in the mind of this man, to unfold his ultimate motive. One concludes that he must have been sustained by the consciousness of being in the right. Only that could have held him against the great desire for fair play which swept over the country. Only the training which an arbitrary will receives by years of consulting first its own personal and commercial ends could have made it strong enough to withstand the demands for social adjustment. He felt himself right from the *commercial* standpoint, and could not see the situation from the *social* standpoint. For years he had gradually accustomed himself to the thought that his motive was beyond reproach; that his attitude to his town was always righteous and philanthropic. Habit held him persistent in this view of the case through all the changing conditions.

The diffused and subtle notion of dignity held by the modern philanthropist bears a curious analogy to the personal barbaric notion of dignity held by Lear. The man who persistently paced the seashore, while the interior of his country was racked with a strife which he alone might have arbitrated, lived out within himself the tragedy of *King Lear*. The shock of disaster upon egotism is apt to produce self-pity. It is possible that his self-pity and loneliness may have been so great and absorbing as to completely shut out from his mind a compunction of derelict duty. He may have been unconscious that men were charging him with a shirking of the issue.

Lack of perception is the besetting danger of the egoist, from whatever cause his egoism arises and envelops him. But, doubtless, philanthropists are more exposed to this danger than any other class of people within the community. Partly because their efforts are overestimated, as no standard of attainment has yet been established, and partly because they are the exponents of a large amount of altruistic feeling with which the community has become equipped and which has not yet found adequate expression, they are therefore easily idealized.

Long ago Hawthorne called our attention to the fact that "philanthropy ruins, or is fearfully apt to ruin, the heart, the rich juices of which God never meant should be pressed violently out, and distilled into alcoholic liquor by an unnatural process; but it should render life sweet, bland and gently beneficent."

One might add to this observation that the muscles of this same heart may be stretched and strained until they lose the rhythm of the common heartbeat of the rest of the world.

Modern philanthropists need to remind themselves of the old definition of greatness: that it consists in the possession of the largest share of the common human qualities and experiences, not in the acquirements of peculiarities and excessive virtues. Popular opinion calls him the greatest of Americans who gathered to himself the largest amount of American experience, and who never forgot when he was in Washington how the "crackers" in Kentucky and the pioneers of Illinois thought and felt, striving to retain their thoughts and feelings, and to embody only the mighty will of the "common people." The danger of professionally attaining to the power of the righteous man, of yielding to the ambition for "doing good," compared to which the ambitions for political position, learning, or wealth are vulgar and commonplace, ramifies throughout our modern life, and is a constant and settled danger in philanthropy.

In so far as philanthropists are cut off from the influence of the *Zeitgeist,* from the code of ethics which rules the body of men, from the great moral life springing from our common experiences, so long as they are "good to people," rather than "with them," they are bound to accomplish a large amount of harm. They are outside of the influence of that great faith which perennially springs up in the hearts of the people, and re-creates the world.

In spite of the danger of overloading the tragedies with moral reflections, a point ought to be made on the other side. It is the weakness in the relation of the employees to the employer, the fatal lack of generosity in the attitude of workmen toward the company under whose exactions they feel themselves wronged.

In reading the tragedy of *King Lear,* Cordelia does not escape our censure. Her first words are cold, and we are shocked by her lack of tenderness. Why should she ignore her father's need for indulgence, and be so unwilling to give him what he so obviously craved? We see in the old king "the overmastering desire of being beloved, which is selfish, and yet characteristic of the selfishness of a loving and kindly nature alone." His eagerness produces in us a strange pity for him, and we are impatient that his youngest and best-beloved child cannot feel this, even in the midst of her search for truth and her newly acquired sense of a higher duty. It seems to us a narrow conception that would break thus abruptly with the past, and would assume that her father had no part in her new life. We want to remind her that "pity, memory and faithfulness are natural ties," and surely as much to be prized as is the development of her own soul. We do not admire the Cordelia "who loves according to her bond" as we later admire the same Cordelia who comes back from France that she may include in her happiness and freer life the father whom she had deserted through her self-absorption. She is aroused to her affection through her pity, but when the floodgates are once open she acknowledges all. It sometimes seems as if only hardship and sorrow could arouse our tenderness, whether in our personal or social relations; that the king, the prosperous man, was the last to receive the justice which can come only through affectionate interpretation. We feel less pity for Lear on his throne than in the storm, although he is the same man, bound up in the same self-righteousness, and exhibiting the same lack of self-control.

As the vision of the life of Europe caught the sight and quickened the pulses of Cordelia, so a vision of the wider life has caught the sight of workingmen. After the vision has once been seen it is impossible to do aught but to press toward its fulfillment. We have all seen it. We are all practically agreed that the social passion of the age is directed toward the emancipation of the wage-worker; that a great accumulation of moral force is overmastering men and making for this emancipation as in another time it has made for the emancipation of the slave; that nothing will satisfy the aroused conscience of men short of the complete participation of the working classes in the spiritual, intellectual and material inheritance of the human race. But just as Cordelia failed to include her father in the scope of her salvation and selfishly took it for herself alone, so workingmen in the dawn of the vision are inclined to claim it for themselves, putting out of their thoughts the old relationships: and just as surely as Cordelia's conscience developed in the new life and later drove her back to her father, where she perished, drawn into the cruelty and wrath which had now become objective and tragic, so the emancipation of working people will have to be inclusive of the employer from the first or it will encounter many failures, cruelties and reactions. It will result not in the position of the repentant Cordelia but in that of King Lear's two older daughters.

If the workingmen's narrow conception of emancipation were fully acted upon, they would hold much the same relationship to their expropriated employer that the two elder daughters held to their abdicated father. When the kingdom was given to them they received it as altogether their own, and were dominated by a sense of possession; "it is ours not yours" was never absent from their consciousness. When Lear ruled the kingdom he had never been without this sense of possession, although he expressed it in indulgence and condescending kindness. His older daughters expressed it in cruelty, but the motive of father and children was not unlike. They did not wish to be reminded by the state and retinue of the old King that he had been the former possessor. Finally, his mere presence alone reminded them too much of that and they banished him from the palace. That a newly acquired sense of possession should result in the barbaric, the incredible scenes of bitterness and murder, which were King Lear's portion, is not without a reminder of the barbaric scenes in our political and industrial relationships, when the sense of possession, to obtain and to hold, is aroused on both sides. The scenes in Paris during the political revolution or the more familiar scenes at the mouths of the mines and the terminals of railways occur to all of us.

The doctrine of emancipation preached to the wage-workers alone runs an awful risk of being accepted for what it offers them, for the sake of the fleshpots, rather than for the human affection and social justice which it involves. This doctrine must be strong enough in its fusing power to touch those who think they lose, as well as those who think they gain. Only thus can it become the doctrine of a universal movement.

The new claim on the part of the toiling multitude, the new sense of responsibility on the part of the well-to-do, arise in reality from the same source. They are in fact the same "social compunction," and, in spite of their widely varying manifestations, logically converge into the same movement. Mazzini once preached, "the consent of men and your own conscience are two wings given you whereby you may rise to God." It is so easy for the good and powerful to think that they can rise by following the dictates of conscience, by pursuing their own ideals, leaving those ideals unconnected with the consent of their fellowmen. The president of the Pullman Company thought out within his own mind a beautiful town. He had power with which to build this town, but he did not appeal to nor obtain the consent of the men who were living in it. The most unambitious reform, recognizing the necessity for this consent, makes for slow but sane and strenuous progress, while the most ambitious of social plans and experiments, ignoring this, is prone to the failure of the model town of Pullman.

The man who insists upon consent, who moves with the people, is bound to consult the feasible right as well as the absolute right. He is often obliged to attain only Mr. Lincoln's "best possible," and often have the sickening sense of compromising with his best convictions. He has to move along with those whom he rules toward a goal that neither he nor they see very clearly till they come to it. He has to discover what people really want, and then "provide the channels in which the growing moral force of their lives shall flow." What he does attain, however, is not the result of his individual striving, as a solitary mountain climber beyond the sight of the valley multitude, but it is underpinned and upheld by the sentiments and aspirations of many others. Progress has been slower perpendicularly, but incomparably greater because lateral.

He has not taught his contemporaries to climb mountains, but he has persuaded the villagers to move up a few feet higher. It is doubtful if personal ambition, whatever may have been its commercial results, has ever been of any value as a motive power in social reform. But whatever it may have done in the past, it is certainly too archaic to accomplish anything now. Our thoughts, at least for this generation, cannot be too much directed from mutual relationships and responsibilities. They will be warped unless we look all men in the face, as if a community of interests lay between, unless we hold the mind open to take strength and cheer from a hundred connections.

To touch to vibrating response the noble fiber in each man, to pull these many fibers, fragile, impalpable and constantly breaking, as they are, into one impulse, to develop that mere impulse through its feeble and tentative stages into action, is no easy task, but lateral progress is impossible without it.

If only a few families of the English-speaking race had profited by the dramatic failure of Lear, much heartbreaking and domestic friction might have been spared. Is it too much to hope that some of us will carefully consider this modern tragedy if perchance it may contain a warning for the troublous times in which we live? By considering the dramatic failure of the liberal employer's plans for his employees we may possibly be spared useless industrial tragedies in the uncertain future which lies ahead of us.

Ray Ginger is chairman of the Committee on American Civilization at Brandeis University. Born in Memphis in 1924, he grew up in the Midwest and was educated at the University of Chicago, the University of Michigan, and Western Reserve. He has taught economics at Western Reserve and business history at Harvard. Before joining the history faculty at Brandeis, he was editor of the *Business History Review* and spent six years as an editor in book publishing. During the summer of 1961 he was visiting research fellow on the History of Kansas City Project.

AMERICAN CENTURY SERIES

Distinguished paperback books in the fields of literature and history, covering the entire span of American culture.